Theresa M Lovehoe £1

THE
HANGING
GARDEN

THE HANGING GARDEN

Creative Displays For Every Garden

SUE FISHER

Photographs by John Glover

HEADLINE

First published in 1995
by HEADLINE BOOK PUBLISHING

1 3 5 7 9 10 8 6 4 2

British Library Cataloguing in Publication Data

Fisher, Sue
    Hanging garden
    I.Title
    635.986

ISBN 0-7472-1211-2

AN EDDISON·SADD EDITION
Edited, designed and produced by
Eddison Sadd Editions Limited
St Chad's Court
146B King's Cross Road
London WC1X 9DH

Phototypeset in Caslon Old Face using
QuarkXPress on Apple Macintosh
Origination by HBM Print PTE Ltd, Singapore
Printed and bound by Jarrold Book Printing Limited,
Thetford, Norfolk, England

HEADLINE BOOK PUBLISHING
A division of Hodder Headline PLC
338 Euston Road
London NW1 3BH

CLIMBER IN A BASKET

Page 1. *Many popular plants for the border can be grown
equally well in a hanging basket. Climbing plants can be woven
around a basket to create a mass of colour, like this beautiful*
Clematis *'Silver Moon'. (p.142)*

A PLATFORM OF FLOWERS

Page 2. *This former railway station provides numerous opportunities
for creating a hanging garden. Baskets hang from supports, tall chimney
pots cluster round the base of a pillar and an old trolley
overflows with pelargoniums. (p.142)*

CONTENTS

Part One

THE EVOLUTION OF THE HANGING GARDEN

Although hanging baskets themselves are very much a product of the twentieth century, the concept of making the most of a limited space by growing plants in raised containers, or training them up walls and frameworks, goes back for thousands of years. Much of the historical development has been in towns and cities where, in order to grow anything, people made many ingenious containers and experimented with different ways of growing plants. Frameworks for climbing plants, on the other hand, were used in gardens of all sizes, both urban and rural.

The art and writings left by great cultures including the ancient Greeks and the Egyptians show that gardens were important for pleasurable as well as practical purposes. Some cultures held the garden in greater regard than others, most notably the Byzantine. The ruling classes of Byzantium considered a garden to be an almost essential part of their lives, to stimulate and delight the senses, and to provide a pleasant place to wander at leisure. From such early beginnings it is possible to chart the development of the hanging garden through history up to the present day.

VICTORIAN CRAFTMANSHIP

Immensely popular during the Victorian era, these wire-work holders are made by twisting several wires together to form a single strand which is then woven into all sorts of decorative and intricate designs. (p.142)

The Hanging Gardens of Babylon – one of the seven ancient wonders of the world – is the best-known historical example of growing plants in containers raised off the ground. According to classical writings the Babylonian king, Nebuchadnezzar II (605–562 BC), created the gardens to please his Persian wife who longed for the lush greenery of her former home. The gardens were said to cover about 1.5 hectares (just over 3 acres) and the planting beds were in the form of raised terraces. Each bed measured approximately 3.5 metres (12 feet) wide and 5 metres (17 feet) high, and they were built up like tiers in a theatre. On each terrace, bundles of reeds, brick tiles and sheets of lead provided a firm and waterproof base for the planting beds and also protected the rooms below. Water for the gardens was drawn from the River Euphrates and pumped up to a cistern on the highest terrace from where it flowed down through pipes and channels to the lower beds. Little is known of the actual planting, though, possibly, it included trees and shrubs such as mimosa and other acacias, cypress and cedar.

Within the Roman Empire gardens developed from as early as the second century BC, initially in Rome. But over the following centuries gardens sprang up throughout Italy and eventually through the whole of the Empire. Pliny the Younger (62–c. 114 AD) wrote of the gardens at his villas at Laurentum near Rome and in Tuscany, north of Rome in the upper valley of the Tiber. His gardens contained sweeping terraces and those at the Tuscan villa included climbing plants such as ivies, some variegated, festooned between plane trees.

The eruption of Mount Vesuvius in 79 AD buried and preserved the prosperous towns of Pompeii and Herculaneum in a way that has enabled archaeologists to excavate the gardens in unparalleled detail. The garden was an integral part of the Roman home, from the largest villas to many of the smaller dwellings and even the living quarters alongside shops. Many containers of plants were used in Roman gardens, and vines were grown to shade balconies. Pots excavated from a villa garden at Oplontis, near Pompeii, were found in pairs at the base of elegant colonnades surrounding a court-

A Victorian artist's impression of the Hanging Gardens of Babylon. Pleasure-gardens played an important part in the culture of ancient civilizations.

yard. According to writings and wall paintings of the time, the pots could well have contained ivy or vines to clothe the columns and the spaces between.

FRAMEWORKS FOR CLIMBERS

Frameworks that were erected specifically for climbing plants have been an essential part of many gardens over thousands of years. The Egyptians used latticed fences, often clad with vines, both along garden boundaries and within the garden itself. Diamond-mesh panels were used in a similar way in Persian gardens. Pliny the Younger had arbours festooned with vines; and in Pompeii a fresco illustrates an elegant arrangement of trellis. Supporting frameworks were not exclusive to the Old World. In the sixteenth century the Spanish explorer Hernando Cortés (1485–1547) found paths that were bordered with plant-covered trellis at the royal gardens of Iztapaplan in Mexico.

Over the past five hundred years or so, climbing-plant supports developed as distinct garden features, particularly pergolas and arbours. They were widely used in the gardens of Renaissance Italy and subsequently throughout Europe. The word *pergola* is Italian, meaning any arbour, bower or close walk of boughs, mainly of vines. In England, arbours were a popular feature of Tudor gardens, often with a grass seat underneath. I can't help thinking that such a spot must have been a very damp place for the fashionable Tudor ladies to rest!

Individual touches were added to these basic structures in different countries. In Portugal, colourful ceramic tiles have been used for centuries to make beautiful decorations, cladding pillars and the supporting frame of pergolas and arbours, as well as to embellish many other parts of the house and garden. The practice of making decorative ceramic tiles, called *azulejo*, was started by the Moors, who invaded the Iberian Peninsula in the eighth century. *Azulejo* comes from the Arabic word *zuleij*, meaning burnt stone, and initially the designs were only geometrical, as regulated by Islamic law. By 1248, with the exception of the Kingdom of Granada, the Moors had been driven out of the Peninsula. However, the practice of tile-making remained. The designs changed and developed to include many different patterns and, under the influence of the Christianity, pictorial subjects. In Portugal today there is a great deal of beautiful and historic tile-work to be seen. One example can be found in the garden of Monserrat, near Sintra, where there are pergolas decorated with tiles. During the fourteenth and fifteenth centuries in England trellis-work, or carpenter's work as it was known, was often featured in gardens. Thomas Hill, in his *Most Briefe and Pleasaunt Treatyse* of 1563, mentions the upkeep of trellis and the virtues or otherwise of using poles of ash, willow and juniper. He goes on to explain how '... the branches of Vine, Mellon, or Cucumber, running and spreading all over, might so shadow and keep both

Decorative trellis-work became something of an art form in seventeenth-century France, illustrated here in a romantic painting by the French artist Hubert Robert (1733–1808).

the heat and Sun from the walkers and sitters thereunder.' In France, the design and construction of elaborate trellis-work reached such a peak of sophistication that it was viewed as an art form and given the name of *trelliage*. In the late sixteenth century, the French gardener Pierre Le Nôtre (*c*.1570–*c*.1610, grandfather of André Le Nôtre), was well-known for his elaborate trellis-work pavilions and arbours which were made of willow and nut poles. Subsequently, trellised structures in many styles became a common feature in gardens of all sizes, and, as well as various woods, materials such as iron and stone were also used for the pillars.

Arbours were often planted with climbing roses, vines, hops and honeysuckles, although elaborate, formal structures were mostly left unplanted to show off their intricate designs. In France, the art of treillage reached its peak in the seventeenth century, particularly in royal gardens such as Versailles and Chantilly where treillage was also used to create design conceits such as *trompe-l'oeil* (literally 'something that deceives the eye'). Trellis panels were mounted on walls, often in conjunction with a painting, to create a false sense of perspective.

The style of formal French gardens, designed to demonstrate human dominance over nature, found less favour in England. It was the landscape gardener Humphry Repton (1725–1818) who brought trellis into the foreground of his designs, often as a device for framing a wider view. He also created rose-gardens edged with arches and trellis to support climbing and rambling roses, anticipating the fashion for roses that would become so popular later in the nineteenth century. Also during the nineteenth century, the increasing interest in a more natural style of gardening brought trellis into widespread use for supporting a whole variety of climbing plants in gardens both large and small. Rustic trellis structures of rough-sawn wood from trees such as larch, were especially favoured during this period.

Arches, pergolas and trellis-work in a wide range of styles were very popular during Victorian and Edwardian times. Wood remained the widest used and most economical material, though wrought iron and wire came very much into vogue. The architect

and garden designer Edwin Lutyens (1869–1944) included pergolas in his designs and developed them into substantial features. The pillars were large and constructed of brick or stone, with timbers running across the top over which the climbing plants could spread. The largest pergola Lutyens designed is at Hestercombe in Somerset, measuring about 72 metres (240 feet) long.

HANGING GARDENS IN TOWNS AND CITIES

The roof terrace has, over the centuries, been a useful area for placing potted plants, particularly in towns where space was limited. John Geometres, the leading tenth-century Byzantine poet, describes his own garden in the centre of Constantinople (now Istanbul) as containing many flowers, shrubs and trees, on balconies and on the roof itself. However, it was during the Italian Renaissance, in the fifteenth century, when interest in roof gardens was aroused. It began in Florence, where Cosimo de' Medici built a roof garden to contain many imported plants. The fashion gradually moved northwards, to Germany, where Cardinal Johann van Lamberg constructed impressive terraces above his home in Passau in the late seventeenth century. Such elaborate constructions were few and far between and they were, of course, the province only of the very wealthy. The roof garden would have to wait for the technical developments of the twentieth century in order to attain wider popularity.

Window-box and balcony gardening, though, were within reach of just about everyone. Just as the urban Romans had grown plants in pots two thousand years ago to satisfy their longing for a little greenery, so did container gardening become ever more popular in the confined spaces of the fast-expanding and overcrowded towns and cities. In our cities today, polluted by the exhaust fumes of millions of cars and lorries, it is easy to believe that we are the first generation badly in need of plants to refresh our environment. But for hundreds of years towns and cities were also subject to pollution of a different kind. Jerry-built houses thrown up in a hurry and packed close together, and no organized system for rubbish or sewage disposal created a stench and squalor it is hard for us to imagine. It is hardly surprising, therefore, that generations of city-dwellers have grown plants in whatever space they could, often with nostalgic longings for the countryside they had been forced to leave in search of work.

The greatest migration of people from the country to the towns was caused by the Industrial Revolution. The development of machinery and its use in manufacturing industries from the eighteenth century onwards created a huge demand for workers in the new and rapidly expanding towns and cities. The money that could be earned in the new mills and industrial areas compared very favourably to the pitifully low agricultural wages of the times. Sadly, people often had no choice in the matter. The Industrial Revolution, by mechanizing and centralizing the production of many items, also brought an end to many small village industries such as weaving, tailoring and spinning. So, with their livelihoods gone and facing poverty and starvation in the countryside, whole families had little alternative but to move to the towns in search of work. William Cowper (1731–1800), a poet with a great love of gardens and the countryside, sympathized with the predicament of these families when he wrote:

> *What are the casements lined with creeping herbs,*
> *The prouder sashes fronted with a range*
> *Of orange, myrtle, or the fragrant weed*
> *The Frenchman's darling**
> *Are they not all proofs,*
> *That man immured in cities, still retains*
> *His inborn, inextinguishable thirst*
> *Of rural scenes, compensates his loss*
> *By supplemental shifts, the best he may?*

(* mignonette)

Through the latter part of the nineteenth century, window-box gardening became more refined. The containers became more decorative, developing from plain, unadorned pots and wooden window-boxes to increasingly ornate items. The trend reached its peak in about 1870, when Shirley Hibberd wrote in *Rustic Adornments for Homes of Taste*: 'Window flower-boxes are now made in a variety of materials and styles, from the humble

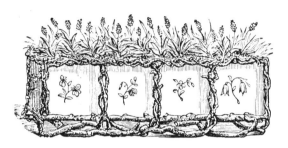

Ornamental window-boxes of the late nineteenth century, illustrated in Rustic Adornments for Homes of Taste *(1870). Gardeners were instructed always to keep their boxes occupied, which necessitated four or five changes of plants in a year.*

trough of deal wood painted stone-colour or dressed with rustic-work, to the richly coloured encaustic tiles, and the equally beautiful and cheap imitations of them. These not only make an end to the ugliness and inconvenience of flower pots, but in them the plants grow far more satisfactorily and require considerably less attention. It is quite common now, and let us rejoice that it is common, to see windows most tastefully embellished with these containers.'

For those who could not afford such decorative items, the gardening writers of the time had plenty of ideas for alternative containers. In *Town and Home Gardening* (1893), Mrs T. Chamberlain outlines how to construct an inexpensive and effective cascading display of plants for balconies: 'The cheapest plan, and one that answers very well, is to procure two tubs (from the grocer or butterman), one wide and low the other narrow and tall. Place the latter inside the shallow one, and plant it first with a group of tall plants and an overhanging edge. Then fill the low outer tub with soil, sloping upwards towards the inner one, so that the appearance, when planted, shall be that of a bank. This again must have drooping plants at the edge to conceal as much as possible of the side.'

A succession of colour for year-round interest was the aim of the planting in these high-profile containers. One window-box planting guide from Shirley Hibberd begins with small, bright, evergreen shrubs for winter followed by masses of small bulbs – snowdrops, crocuses, hyacinths and early tulips – mixed so the leaves of the early bulbs formed a green background for the later ones. For summer, recommended plants include pelargoniums, calceolarias, lobelias and fuchsias, though gold- and silver-foliage plants appear to have been out of favour for window-boxes. Mixed asters or dwarf chrysanthemums are suggested for autumn, followed by evergreens again for winter. In late autumn the displays can be enlivened by red-berried skimmias and also by the colourful orange berries of *Solanum pseudocapsicum*, a tender plant which would last only until the first frosts.

An example of the type of balcony and window garden which was fashionable in towns and cities in the nineteenth century. Climbing plants have been trained up either side of the window.

With four or five changes of plants in a year, it was hardly surprising that many nurseries sprang up to cope with the flourishing demand for colourful town-house frontages. But sadly this floriferous state of affairs was not to last. As the cost of labour and materials increased, so did the prices charged by nurserymen. These factors, coupled with the unwillingness and, indeed, the inability of the well-off homeowners to get their hands dirty, eventually brought an end to such displays. A mere twenty-three years after Shirley Hibberd praised the beauty of the City's window-boxes, Mrs T. Chamberlain lamented the decline of London's floral decoration. On one of her infrequent visits to the capital she saw: '… several houses where, a few seasons back, that the window-boxes were gay and the balcony had afforded a green retreat, all such efforts had completely ceased.' She regretfully concluded: 'Experience proves to me that the falling-off in the floral appearance of the West-end is attributable to two causes – the greed of the professional nurseryman and the ignorance of the amateur.'

THE ADVENT OF THE HANGING BASKET

The latter half of the nineteenth century saw the appearance of the first lightweight wire hanging baskets, the making of which became possible due to important technological developments. Prior to this time, blacksmiths could construct ornamental items such as gates out of wrought iron, but due to the amount of carbon contained within the iron, it was too brittle to be made into fine, decorative containers. Also, the sheer weight of a wrought iron container would have made it impractical to suspend from brackets or other supports.

Consequently, raised containers of plants were few and far between. Wicker baskets placed on sawn-off tree trunks or tripods of wood were used to break up large expanses of lawn. These rustic baskets were informally planted with scrambling climbers such as *Asarina barclayana* and *Eccremocarpus scaber* – the Chilean glory vine, ferns, fuchsias, and ivy-leaved pelargoniums. Such informal plantings were in contrast to the rigid and brightly coloured formality of the bedding schemes that were all the rage with the Victorians.

It was the invention of the Bessemer converter that made it possible to make wire hanging baskets. In 1856, Henry Bessemer announced he had developed a process to produce steel cheaply and in quantity by blowing air through molten pig iron to burn away the impurities. His converter was rather like a huge concrete mixer, in that it was tipped in order to be loaded with between twenty-five and fifty tons of molten pig iron and then moved upright. Air was blown through holes in the base and forced up through the molten iron. Carbon was removed in the form of a gas, carbon monoxide, and other impurities combined with oxygen and separated out as slag which was left behind when the molten iron was tipped out of the converter. The resulting pure iron could be drawn into fine wire, by pulling rods of the material about 6 millimetres (¼ inch) in diameter through a series of dies, each one slightly smaller than the last. Within a few years, Bessemer's production works at Sheffield was producing in the region of one million tons of steel annually.

The great advantage of wire was its flexibility which enabled it to be bent and woven into all sorts of items. With the Victorians' love of ornament, woven wire containers soon became all the rage for the home. Hanging baskets, racks, jardinières and flower stands of all shapes and sizes, often beautiful and intricate in their design, were to be found in fashionable houses. Books of the time instructed owners always to keep their flower stands 'bright, clean and gay'. As soon as a plant went out of bloom, it would be replaced with another. The succession of plants included roses, pelargoniums, fuchsias, azaleas and camellias. Genistas and heaths were also mentioned, presumably the frost-tender species such as *Cytisus* × *spachianus* (now *Genista* × *spachiana*) and Cape heaths such as *Erica hyemalis*.

These wire containers were only suitable for the house and conservatory. The material would quickly rust if left outside unless painted regularly. It was not until the introduction of the galvanizing process in the 1870s, whereby the completed item could be dipped into a bath of molten zinc and so become rust-proofed, that wire containers could be used for outdoor decoration with any safety.

Then as now, these hand-crafted and labour-intensive items could only be afforded by those with money to spare, though the fact that workers of the time were poorly paid obviously made wire containers less expensive at first. However, the economy began to decline during the early part of the twentieth century and this, coupled with the growing demand by workers to be paid a living wage, led to the gradual disappearance of many labour-intensive businesses including wire-working. However, one has survived and continues to flourish. The firm of James Gilbert & Son in Acton, West London, has been going for four generations.

Today the company continues to make hundreds of wire-work items to designs from its catalogue, first published in the 1870s. Sometimes items sold many years ago will resurface for restoration, their

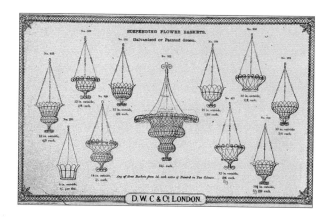

Woven wire baskets, from the catalogue of James Gilbert & Son, were all the rage with the Victorians. The firm still makes baskets to these designs today.

present owners tracking down the company from the name engraved on the baskets or an old receipt. In this way a dozen hanging baskets, bought for the Ritz Hotel in 1906, were returned recently for refurbishment. Staff at the hotel had discovered the company's name and looked it up in the telephone directory.

THE MODERN ROOF GARDEN

The roof garden began to play an increasingly prominent role in new buildings in towns and cities. The development of strong, load-bearing materials, such as reinforced steel, along with very efficient waterproofing agents put the construction of large roof gardens within affordable reach.

But initially, the roof-garden concept had to be taken up by architects. The controversial Swiss architect Le Corbusier (1887–1965) was one of the first to give them high priority in order to improve the urban quality of life. He included roof gardens in many of his housing projects, such as the Pessac estate of 1925 and the Unité d'Habitation at Marseilles, built just after the Second World War. However, it was the American architect Frank Lloyd Wright (1869–1959) who really developed the theme of integrating nature with man-made structures. His designs softened the hard, horizontal lines of buildings and balconies with cascading curtains of foliage, such as at the Imperial Hotel in Tokyo, and Falling Water, the Kaufmann house, built in Pennsylvania in 1936.

Today in the United States there are many beautifully planted terraces and roof gardens, often in public areas such as shopping malls, atriums and multi-storey car parks. As pressure on urban land increases, along with the growing realization of the importance of plants and gardens, both as natural clean-air producers and as morale boosters for overcrowded town-dwellers, so roof gardens are increasing in number around the world.

THE HANGING GARDEN TODAY

It was mass production of materials, principally wire and plastic, that finally brought hanging baskets within affordable reach of the ordinary gardener. Plastic, a product derived from petroleum, was originally dubbed 'the miracle material of a thousand uses' when Leo Baekeland (1863–1944) patented a synthetic resin that he called Bakelite in 1907. Plastic is now used to make many different designs of hanging basket, as well as numerous other plant containers.

Through the first half of the twentieth century, the decorative side of gardening was almost eclipsed by devastating events. The First World War which broke out in 1914 caused far-reaching social and economic upheaval culminating in the worldwide slump during the 1930s and the outbreak of the Second World War.

During the Second World War, food rationing was introduced in Britain as sea and air import routes were severed. Then town as well as country gardens were turned over to the production of vegetables and fruit, as the nation was exhorted to 'dig for victory'. Every available resource was poured into the war effort. My mother remembers all the elegant Victorian cast-iron railings in her street being taken away to be melted down in the weapons' factories. When peace reigned again, however, some of the redundant equipment of war could be pressed into use in the garden. Another of my mother's recollections is of seeing soldiers' and air raid wardens' helmets planted and hung up as makeshift hanging baskets!

Books published just before and after the Second World War demonstrate the growing enthusiasm for window-box and hanging-basket gardening, and the ever-increasing range of plants used in them. W. E. Shewell-Cooper wrote in *Home, Window and Roof Gardening* (1938) that 'it might almost be said that it is our national duty to cultivate window-boxes' (and presumably hanging-baskets as well) in order to improve the environment. He also recommends mixed baskets as being more effective than one-colour baskets or those filled with only one type of plant. His chosen plants include asparagus fern and golden-veined honeysuckle (presumably *Lonicera japonica* 'Aureoreticulata'), variegated periwinkle, nasturtiums and *Campanula isophylla*, plus the ever-popular ivy-leaved pelargoniums, fuchsias, begonias and lobelias. Scented plants including night-scented stocks, tobacco plants and heliotropes were recommended for baskets, though these tall plants must have looked rather straggly in such a situation. *Saxifraga stolonifera* seems to have been popular with later writers. Treated as a house plant in colder areas, this handsome foliage plant will actually withstand some frost. Its common name of mother-of-thousands comes from the numerous young plantlets, borne on thin stems, which dangle beneath the basket to make an attractive display.

In the gardening books of the 1950s, the range of recommended plants widens to include some less common species. Among those listed are *Fuchsia procumbens* with its small, upright, yellow flowers with purple sepals and bright blue pollen; *Cereus flagelliformis*, the rat's tail cactus; *Lantana montevidensis*, a mat-forming species with rose-purple flowers; *Lotus* species; *Nierembergia* and *Sanvitalia*; and foliage plants like *Soleirolia soleirolii* (intriguingly known as mind-your-own-business or baby's tears) and *Selaginella*.

Summer-interest plants predominate, though spring flowers are also mentioned. As well as old faithfuls like arabis, forget-me-nots and primroses, there are suggestions for planting baskets with bulbs such as crocuses to create a mass of colour, using them in the sides as well as at the top. I have created similar plantings with grape hyacinths, which look absolutely gorgeous.

Although wooden and plastic baskets are referred to, wire baskets lined with moss, or with polythene pierced at the base for drainage, were the principal type that writers of the early post-war years recommended. Turf is sometimes mentioned as a liner – presumably grass-side in! Some ingenious, though time-consuming, ideas were put forward to improve the watering of wire baskets. In August 1967, one correspondent to *Gardeners' Chronicle* magazine described how to create a rim for wire baskets which would retain water long enough to soak the compost thoroughly. He recommended combining moist clay with chopped straw to form a dough-like mixture which could then be moulded around the rim of a moss-lined basket and left to dry.

Although all these plants and containers were available through small shops and nurseries, it was the advent of the garden centre concept in the 1950s that made gardening supplies easily accessible to everyone. With plants, composts, containers and other sundries all available in one place, gardening was set to flourish as never before.

Fortunately for all of us, the planting of hanging baskets and window boxes has not been confined solely to the private gardener. More and more shops, businesses, and indeed whole towns, are creating attractive floral frontages, and these displays inspire and lift the spirits of customers and passers-by. In some European countries, window-boxes overflowing with gaily coloured plants can be seen almost everywhere. Even the smallest French village has a few window-boxes filled with pink and red pelargoniums, and in the more picturesque towns popular with tourists, the displays are often superb. Towns like Santillina del Mar in northern Spain, where I have seen balconies and house fronts absolutely covered with cascading trails of flowers and foliage, are worth visiting just for the plants.

Nowadays, there is a huge range of plants and containers to choose from in the many garden centres, as well as labour-saving devices such as automatic watering systems. As gardens become smaller and home-owners more affluent, product manufacturers have risen to the challenge of small-space gardening with a will. They have created a multitude of containers from traditional hanging baskets and wall pots to hanging growing bags in the form of swags and flower pouches. Many of these are designed for cheapness and practicality rather than being aesthetically pleasing, with the view that a well-planted container should soon be hidden under a cascade of plant growth. However, there are also many beautiful containers made of terracotta, wrought iron, and even woven wire baskets based on Victorian designs. Similarly, there is a wide variety of supports available for climbing plants. From basic plastic-covered wire rose arches to rustic wooden pergolas and wrought-iron gazebos, there is something for everyone's taste and budget.

A hanging garden brings plants so close to the house that the two almost merge. So arranged, the plants are far more approachable and intimate than those in more distant borders. Around my house, a mass of golden bidens can be seen through the front window, seeming to fill the living-room with sunshine. At the shadier rear a summer jasmine rambles along the wall, its perfume drifting in through open windows. A few minutes spent tending my containers – watering, deadheading and feeding – are one of the best ways I know of winding down at the end of a busy day.

I find it immensely encouraging that so many people are now discovering the pleasures of this type of gardening, however limited their space may be. With so many ways of creating a hanging garden, the sky really is the limit today!

Part Two

THE PLANTING DISPLAYS

G*ardeners of today have* *unparalleled opportunities to garden into the vertical dimension. As space becomes ever more precious, often the only way to make more of our gardens is to go up, or down. We have house walls, often two storeys high, and boundary walls and fences, all of which can support plants in hanging baskets and wall pots, as well as lots of climbing plants. To me, the overwhelming bonus of growing plants in this way is the sheer flexibility. In fact, you don't even need to have a garden in order to enjoy some beautiful hanging baskets and window-boxes. Trailing and climbing plants can be fitted into the smallest space, and container gardening is something that is open to absolutely everyone, regardless of experience or location.*

In The Hanging Garden *you'll not only find some superb displays of traditional trailers and climbers, but also many innovative plantings of new and less common plants, sometimes in unusual containers. As well as giving me the chance to put some of my own ideas into practice, this book has also drawn together the creative ideas of a number of top professional gardeners and growers. I would like to thank them all for contributing so much of their time and expertise. I hope you will be inspired to re-create some of our displays in your own garden. If so, turn to the final part of the book to find out the secrets of each planting.*

PLANT-COVERED PUB

A spectacular collection of summer bedding – principally pelargoniums, petunias and busy lizzies – growing in hanging baskets, wall baskets, a window-box and various individual pots. (p.142)

BASKETS AND BOXES
Annuals and bedding plants

he vagaries of fashion have dictated that the popularity of bedding plants has waxed and waned for well over a hundred years. Their great heyday was during the latter half of the nineteenth century when the Victorian craze for 'bedding out' was at its height and influenced the planting of virtually all public and private gardens of that time. Most garden borders were planted exclusively with bedding plants, which were often laid out in intricate patterns and designs.

But towards the end of the nineteenth century the wheel of change was starting to turn. Typical of many gardeners' reactions was that of Henry Bright, who wrote in *A Year in a Lancashire Garden* (1879): 'For the ordinary bedding out of ordinary gardens I have a real contempt. It is at once gaudy and monotonous. A garden is left bare for eight months in the year, that for the four hottest months there shall be a blaze of the hottest colours.'

Perhaps it was this backlash that has coloured the attitudes to bedding plants that a fair few people still hold today: that such plants are gaudy, garish, and somewhat beyond the realms of good taste. But, setting aside the question of taste, which after all is a personal matter, the beauty of such plants is that there really is something for everyone, with flower colours ranging from the softest pastels to flaming oranges and fiery reds, bicolours included. For the hanging garden, bedding plants really are essential for long-lasting seasonal colour.

The real value of these seasonal plants today lies in their suitability for all sorts of containers, rather than bedding out garden borders. And by far and away the most versatile of all containers are hanging baskets and window-boxes. In flats or town houses without a garden, or where the frontage of a house has no ground space for planting, such containers make it possible to have a stunning display of plants all year round. Hanging baskets can be suspended from stout brackets screwed onto a wall. Window-boxes can sit on deep windowsills or, if the sill is not wide enough, on some L-shaped brackets or a purpose-built shelf. Either way, secure fixture and stability must be priorities, especially if the containers are above ground floor level, because no passer-by is likely to relish a container of plants landing on their head! In such situations, it is a good idea to water plants during the times when there are few passing pedestrians, and to install a drip tray.

With a few stylish exceptions at the more expensive end of the range, hanging baskets are strictly functional. The secret of successful baskets is to cram them full of plants so the actual container is hidden from view in a very short space of time. A similar principle applies to window-boxes. In the latter case, it is important to remember that you will see the planting from indoors as well as outside, so it needs to look good from all angles. With so many plants living in such a small space, regular watering and feeding is essential, and full details of these tasks are given on pages 139 and 140.

TRADITIONAL FAVOURITES

Petunias, pelargoniums and lobelias – favourite summer plants that give a reliable and sensational display. A whitewashed wall provides a perfect backdrop to the rich colours and velvety textures. (p.143)

The mainstays of summer containers are pelargoniums (incorrectly, referred to as bedding geraniums), fuchsias, petunias, busy lizzies, lobelias and pansies. The colour range offered collectively by these plants is enormous, and there are a wealth of different types to choose from. For example, among pelargoniums alone there are trailing ivy-leaved kinds; the cascade, or the Balcon series, so popular for use in window-boxes in many European countries, especially in Switzerland; plus bedding pelargoniums of compact, upright form, ideal as a centrepiece for a container. In addition, there are some choice, less usual kinds with handsome scented foliage which can smell variously of lemon, cedar, pine, rose or peppermint.

The shift in interest from the bedding out of garden borders to hanging baskets and tubs has encouraged plant breeders to look for new cultivars and hybrids. Developments in breeding plants to suit containers have concentrated both on compact, upright, bushy plants for the centres, and those with a vigorous but lax, trailing habit ideal for covering the sides of baskets and tall pots.

Some stunning new forms of old favourites have been introduced in recent years and these are fast becoming popular with both private and professional gardeners. There are New Guinea *Impatiens* which have larger flowers than those of their smaller cousins, with the added bonus of bold, handsome foliage, and a greater tolerance of hot, sunny conditions. Surfinia petunias are real eye-catchers, with an enormous number of flowers borne on vigorous, scandent stems. There is even a trailing antirrhinum, *A. pendula*, with stems that extend up to a metre long (about 3 ft), covered with 'snapdragon' flowers in a mixture of colours from white, through yellow and pink, with a touch of scarlet.

The plant breeders are constantly looking for both new cultivars and improved forms of existing ones. Alan Miles of Colegrave Seeds, a British wholesale seed company, lists the main qualities on which a plant is assessed: 'We look at flower colour, especially with regard to new shades, flower size, number of blooms per plant and length of flower production. Good foliage is important, and we also look for colours such as bronzed or variegated leaves. Then there is the need for overall vigour and a good habit, plus the ability to perform well in a garden situation to be sure that the plant gives good value for money.'

One way the gardener can be sure of choosing the top plant from all these new ones is to look for those that have been given an award by Fleuroselect, a European organization which tests new flower seed selections. Plants are grown on trial grounds throughout Europe, so they can be assessed on how they grow in varied conditions. At each place, judges award points on individual plant performance, and at the end of the season, the points from all the different trial grounds are totalled up. Those plants that have performed well and consistently get a high score are given a Fleuroselect award. A few of the most outstanding performers are given a coveted gold medal.

SOFT AND SUBTLE PARTNERS

A delicate combination which is simple to achieve – deep pink busy lizzies above a cloud of blue lobelia – ideal for lightening a shady spot. (p.143)

Nicotiana 'Havana Appleblossom' and *N.* 'Havana Lime Green', *Pelargonium* 'Orange Appeal', *Impatiens* 'Mega Orange Star' and *Viola* 'Velour Blue' have all won the coveted award. The USA has a similar system: the All Americas selections.

Though summer containers still tend to claim the greater part of the gardener's interest, winter displays are making a steady advance. There is an increasing range of dependable plants available from autumn for display until spring. Winter-flowering pansies were amongst the first plants to be used on a wide scale. They have recently been joined by ornamental cabbages and kales with red, pink or white leaves. A few dwarf bulbs such as crocus, dwarf daffodils or tulips can be added for spring colour. Winter containers need plenty of foliage for structure and extra colour. In addition to the reliable ivies with all their bright variegations, it is possible to use young shrubs such as *Lonicera nitida* 'Baggesen's Gold', *Santolina*, *Helichrysum italicum* subsp. *serotinum* – the curry plant, and *Euonymus fortunei* cultivars such as 'Emerald 'n' Gold', as well as conifers. In the spring, the shrubs and conifers can be moved into larger containers or planted out in the garden.

When it comes to choosing your plants, it is well worth experimenting with different colour combinations in the garden in exactly the same way as you would in the home. After all, each room is usually decorated to a colour scheme, and as containers are mostly close to the house, it is a good idea to extend the same courtesy to them. If you are unsure about where to begin, start by taking a look at the building itself, which will be the backdrop for your plant displays. Think of the colours that will look best against it. For example, a wall of brand new, bright red brick would be an excellent contrast to white and pale, pastel shades such as creams, pale blues and yellows, but much less so to deep pinks and reds. Correspondingly, white and cream walls ensure dark, rich colours stand out to perfection.

For the plants themselves, try restricting the number of colours in a group of containers. A limited range will give a much more effective overall appearance than lots of different colours all jumbled together. If you are dubious about putting several

NEW BUSY LIZZIES

New Guinea Impatiens, *with their large flowers and bold, often colourful foliage, have enough impact to be planted on their own. This hybrid is 'Rhapsody'. (p.143)*

different plants in one container, bear in mind that single-plant hanging baskets can look spectacular; for examples of this see the *Begonia* 'Illumination' on page 27, or *Pelargonium* 'Ville de Dresden' on page 22. Single-plant containers can always be grouped together for a contrasting effect; one of the beauties of containers is that they can be mixed and matched, and moved around to ring the changes.

Colour theming of bedding plants has developed enormously in popularity. Whereas a few years ago most plants and seeds were sold in mixed packs, it is now easy to buy them in their separate colours. Choice of colours is very much a personal preference, so before you go shopping for seeds and plants, it is a good idea to decide on the sort of effect you want to create – hot and fiery, cool and pastel, strong but subtle. So regardless of the dictates of fashion you can end up with a planting scheme that pleases you, and which will give you plenty of colour for months on end.

HIGH SUMMER STYLE

Opposite. *A traditional basket planting at its very best. Jane Lees follows the golden rules of hanging-basket planting: cram the container chock-full of plants, then give them plenty of food and water, and remove dead blooms every day. This is one of about twenty baskets hung outside the Brickmaker's Arms in Windlesham, Surrey, one of the many British pubs with a display of spectacular containers. (p.143)*

PELARGONIUM CASCADE

Above. *Trailing, ivy-leaved pelargoniums always make a first-class display in a hanging basket, whether they are mixed in with other plants or, as in this case, grown on their own. There is a huge colour range too: from soft pastels such as this 'Ville de Dresden', with palest pink flowers, to many shades of red, purple and pink, as well as bicolours. All pelargoniums thrive in a sunny site. (p.143)*

DECORATIVE PERGOLA

Left. *More of Jane Lees' baskets, hung from a stout wooden pergola. Such garden structures are useful supports for climbing plants and, with the addition of hanging baskets, can be transformed into a hanging garden. (p.143)*

A DELICATE COMBINATION

Above. *An enchanting collection of blue and creamy yellow pansies, white verbena and a pink fuchsia, spangled with golden violas. At the top are shoots of* Bidens *with its yellow daisy flowers and ferny foliage. The silvery leaves of helichrysum with their bold outline prevent the overall planting from looking too fussy. (p.143)*

LOW-LEVEL BASKETS

Opposite. *Give hanging baskets a new look by suspending them at a different level to normal. These Hi-lo devices are most useful to lower a basket temporarily for easy watering and maintenance, but here the displays have been left down to create an unusual effect. (p.144)*

BOUNTIFUL BEGONIA

Above. *Trailing begonias are most often seen mixed in with other plants, but Cascade begonias such as the one illustrated make a fine display on their own. This selection of the Illumination F1 hybrids produces long trailing stems covered with abundant flowers which contrast beautifully with the large, dark leaves. (p.144)*

AN UNUSUAL LINING

Opposite. *An autumn basket brings welcome colour as the days become shorter and darker. But what interests me most about this basket is its lining. Take a closer look, and you can see that it is made by using green conifer clippings rather than the usual lining of moss or a manufactured material. These foliage clippings are ideal for autumn and winter baskets because they will stay green, although in summer they would probably turn brown fairly quickly. (p.144)*

SHADES OF SILVER

Above. *A background of dark brick and deep brown wood calls for pale colours, and the ice cool tones of helichrysum foliage and white busy lizzies are set off to perfection by such a background. Touches of blue brings the basket to life. They are provided by the blue-mauve flowers of the Swan River daisy, or* Brachyscome, *trailing underneath, and a variegated* Felicia *in the centre. Compact, bushy plants like* Felicia *are ideal for the centre of a hanging basket as they give plenty of height and substance without becoming too tall and rangy. (p.144)*

WARM WINDOW-BOX

Left. *A perfectly blended mixture of foliage gives a warm, greeny gold backing to a collection of mainly red flowers. The eye-catching, pointed, variegated leaves are those of* Tradescantia, *widely used as a house plant but, for some reason, comparatively rarely grown in outdoor containers. Here it rubs shoulders with other popular foliage plants such as variegated ivy and golden creeping Jenny. A dwarf conifer at each end of the window-box helps to give the planting definition.* (p.144)

TAKING THE CHILL OFF

Above. *Foliage features strongly here, but it is the scalloped green and white leaves of the variegated ground ivy that tends to draw the eye. A useful plant for all forms of hanging gardens, it quickly develops long dangling leafy trails over a metre (3 or 4 feet) long, and the leaves give off a fresh, pungent smell when crushed. The touch of pale yellow provided by lemon yellow petunias and lime green helichrysum stops the overall effect from looking too white and icy cold.* (p.145)

ANYTHING GOES
Annuals and bedders in unusual containers

P art of the fun of container gardening is that there is literally no limit to the different sorts of containers that can be pressed into service. There is an amazing range of items on sale that have been produced especially for creating a hanging garden, such as pouches and swags, wall pots and troughs, as well as tall, elegant urns. But it goes without saying that few gardeners have unlimited cash to spend on tailor-made pots. One of the aspects of gardening I enjoy most is to hunt down all sorts of cheap or throw away things that can be planted up and arranged to make an unusual and attractive display – and very often a real talking-point. Junk shops, reclamation merchants, car-boot and garage sales and even the small classified adverts in local papers, can all provide rich pickings for the resourceful gardener.

My great ally in the creation of some out-of-the-ordinary displays has been Hampshire nurseryman Brian Smith, a specialist in bedding plants and former chairman of the British Bedding and Pot Plant Association. He has created lots of superb plantings in some very unusual containers indeed: worn-out boots, an old toilet hijacked before it reached the tip, and a pensioned-off milk churn – all have been given a new lease of life. A look around the local craft-market led him to discover a man who paints

LAVATORY HUMOUR

There really is no limit to the things that can be adopted for plant containers. This old toilet, filled with a stunning mixture of busy lizzies and foliage plants, is perfect for cheering up a shady corner. (p.145)

buckets and watering cans in the colourful designs seen on traditional old canal boats. Brian emphasizes: 'The important thing is to get away from the conventional idea that plants must be in a round or square pot, or a trough. They can go in just about anything, and trailing plants are excellent as they can be used to disguise any less attractive containers. For successful plantings, it's important that flower colour complements foliage colour, and to keep the various plant habits in balance.'

Brian's zeal and enthusiasm for bedding plants is boundless, and he is already a familiar face to gardeners in the south of England, where he has held a series of bedding 'road-shows' for several years. The practical aspects of planting and maintenance are dressed up in jokes to get the message over without being tedious, and his favourite analogy is that plants are like people – they need tender loving care, feeding and watering … and occasionally dead-heading. Other topics are covered in a similar vein, such as the necessity for good drainage: 'Would *you* like to stand with your feet in a bucket of water?' Or on over-firming compost: 'Plants are like people, they need to breathe!' After rounding off with a high-speed, humorous planting demonstration, the audience leaves, brim-full of enthusiasm.

As a confirmed plant addict, I need no convincing that plants are excellent value for money, but Brian is often asked whether bedding plants are worth buying because they only last for one season. His reply is: 'Look at the price of a pack of annuals that are planted out in late spring and flower solidly through to the autumn, and work out the cost per week – then compare it to something like an ice cream which is gone in minutes.' I know which I would rather have!

There is a range of annuals to suit every pocket, and all the traditional bedding plants, such as pelargoniums and fuchsias mentioned in the previous chapter, adapt well to any sort of container provided it is well-drained. But whilst exploring a wider range of containers, it is also worth looking at some trailing annuals that can be raised from seed, and which offer exceptional value if you are gardening on a budget.

A leaf through a few seed catalogues will turn up many tempting trailers. Here are a few examples for some dazzling colour. Mesembryanthemums – popularly known as 'mezzies' or Livingstone daisies – are succulent-leaved plants with day-glow bright flowers that do well in a sunny, well-drained spot. Enjoying similar conditions is *Sanvitalia procumbens* which bears orange-yellow flowers with a large black 'eye'.

Then, of course, there are nasturtiums which are just about the easiest of all annuals to grow. No need to bother with raising them in pots and transplanting them out – just push the seeds into the compost and watch them grow! Their speed and reliability of growth makes them ideal for filling any unexpected gaps in hanging baskets too – simply push in a few seeds through the mesh and the nasturtiums will soon catch up with the other plants.

As well as all these brilliant colours, there are plenty of trailers in softer shades. Still with nasturtiums, 'Strawberries and Cream' is a new cultivar with creamy yellow petals marked at the base with spots of red. *Asarina procumbens* has light yellow, trumpet-shaped flowers and does well in shade. *Nolana* 'Shooting Star' also has trumpet-shaped flowers but of pale blue, while *N.* 'Blue Bird' is a deeper blue with a striking creamy white centre. *Nierembergia* 'Mont Blanc' bears masses of enchanting little flowers, pure white with a yellow eye – though I found that slugs adore it, so confine it to hanging baskets well out of their reach.

Compact annuals with an upright habit can be used in the centre of baskets and containers. Increasingly there are new, dwarf forms of popular plants becoming available that fit the bill, such as

A LOAD OF COBBLERS

Brian Smith's old work boots are given a new lease of life, filled with distinctive foliage plants, including trailing bugle, sedum, variegated ivy and coleus. (p.146)

cornflowers *Centaurea* 'Florence White' and *Centaurea* 'Blue Baby', and the tobacco plant *Nicotiana* 'Apple Blossom'.

In addition to flowers, it is worth bearing in mind plants with attractive fruit. Ornamental gourds produce vigorous sprawling stems and are a handsome curiosity for a sunny spot. Their inedible fruits come in all manner of colours and shapes – the aptly named cultivar 'Choose your Weapon' gives some indication of what to expect. Gourds are closely related to marrows and require similar treatment. That is, sow the seeds in pots during mid-spring and plant out when all danger of frost is past. A rich, moisture-retentive soil gives the best results. At the end of the season ripe gourds can be dried in

Trails of gold- and silver-variegated ivy cascade down from a raised bed on to the upturned faces of colourful ornamental cabbages and pansies to cover this patio corner with autumn colour. The pansies are from the Ultima range and should flower from autumn to spring, weather permitting. Their flower colours have been chosen to tone with those of the cabbages. There is a mixture of containers clustered together – an old milk churn to provide height, a hand-painted bucket and watering-can, as well as a conventional terracotta pot. (p.146)

the sun and then brought indoors to display in a dish or with dried flowers. The fruits can even be painted with clear varnish to give a glossy finish. The colour of the yellow fruits in particular seem to 'hold' the sunlight they have absorbed during the summer.

I love reading old books and magazines to see what was grown in gardens of the past and how the plants were used. However, it is as well not to follow some tips without a second thought – such as Mrs C. W. Earle's bedding plant recommendations in *Pot-Pourri from a Surrey Garden* (1897). She wrote, that 'for beauty of growth and foliage there are few things as lovely as the common Hemp plant

(*Cannabis sativa*)'. This plant, also known as mari-juana, is not to be recommended for bedding if you want to stay on the right side of the law!

Still, on the whole, gardeners are law-abiding – so long as the search for unusual containers doesn't actually lead to pinching them. Using a mixture of containers for plants is just one way of developing a garden that looks stunningly individual. Take this one stage further by grouping the containers carefully according to height or raising some on bricks, upturned pots, a low wall or a window-sill. Then, once they are planted and growth gets under way, a waterfall effect of flowing foliage will result – a hanging garden on the ground.

INNER CITY HANGING GARDEN

This incredible, flowery hanging garden is an absolute masterpiece, and a prime example of 'where there's a will, there's a way'. Fey Hasan has crammed about four hundred ordinary plastic pots full of flowers around her first-floor balcony. The pots, ranged in rows either side of the window, are sitting on wooden shelves with a rail at the front to hold them securely. The front of the balcony is covered with plastic mesh on to which individual pots are wired using recycled coat hangers. Only a stone's throw from the roar and fumes of traffic on London's King's Cross Road, this house front is an oasis of summer colour. (p.146)

LONDON BOROUGH OF ISLING
PERCY
CIRCUS W.C

LEAFY PICTURE FRAME

Opposite. *A niche has been clipped out of this hedge to make a perfect frame for an urn filled with lewisias and ivy, so good for trailing down a tall container. Although lewisias are perennial plants, I find that they tend to give a good show for only one year in a container. (p.147)*

HOME FROM THE SEA

Above. *Its seafaring days over, this old boat on the Norfolk coast has found a new role in life, full to the gunwales with a colourful froth of nasturtiums. These vigorous annuals are easy to grow from seed and, set against a plain dark background of brick and ivy, they look spectacular as they spill over onto the gravel 'sea'. (p.147)*

ANCIENT URN

Opposite. *The handsome Grecian urns shown on these pages, both belonging to Lynda Brown, were used to store olive oil for many years. Rather than filling such* massive pots with compost, a large flowerpot has been wedged in the top. Using a smaller container in this way makes it possible to start off the plants under cover. (p.147)*

HIGH ABOVE THE HERBS

Above. *In the middle of Lynda's herb garden, the large urn, painted white, makes an excellent focal point. Although foliage plants usually adorn the sides of containers, here the bright flowers of fuchsia* trail down to show off their blooms. At the base, the golden leaved hardy Fuchsia 'Genii' reaches up, its colour echoing the lime-green foliage of helichrysum planted in the top of the urn. (p.147)*

UNDERSTUDY INTO STAR

Opposite. *Trailing lobelia is used so much as an infill in plant in baskets and pots that it is rarely given a chance to take centre stage. But doesn't it look spectacular on its own? Three different colours are* *planted together in a hanging 'swag bag' which is simply hooked onto the wooden trellis mounted on the wall. Alternatively, massed lobelia would look equally good overflowing from a hanging basket. (p.148)*

HIGH-LEVEL WALL BASKET

Above. *Caught in the last rays of the afternoon sun, the slender bells of* Fuchsia *'Cascade' stand out against a background of soft greens and golds. The ferny foliage belongs to* Sambucus racemosa *'Tenuifolia',* *a small shrub often described as the 'poor man's Japanese maple' though I find it every bit as handsome. It can only stay in this wall basket for a few months before being moved on to a roomier home. (p.148)*

BAGS OF BUSY LIZZIES

Opposite. *Hanging growing bags are ideal for distracting the eye from ugly objects, like this telegraph pole. Busy lizzies are ideal for these bags. Plant them early in the season using young plants or starter plants known as 'plugs'.* (p.148)

GARLAND OF BRIGHT EYES

Left. *One of my favourite busy lizzies is* Accent *'Bright Eye', with pink flowers and a dark pink centre.* (p.148)

TOOTHY SMILE

Below. *Who could fail to be cheered by this welcoming grin on the wall, created by a gleaming line of white busy lizzies between the dark red 'lips'.* (p.148)

WHAT GOES UP ...
Climbers and trailers

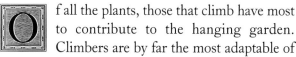

O f all the plants, those that climb have most to contribute to the hanging garden. Climbers are by far the most adaptable of all the hardy garden plants, not least because what goes up can, of course, come down. In most cases the stems of a climbing plant will naturally cascade down once they have reached the top of the support, but these trailing properties can be taken one step further. They can be exploited to the full if the plant is put in a raised container such as a hanging basket or a tall pot, and left unsupported to create a dramatic cascade of flowers and foliage. Similarly, climbers have great potential on steep banks. Such sites can be transformed by planting climbers to ramble downhill and provide a more exciting alternative to grass, which is so awkward to mow on steep slopes. Coupled with a bark mulch to keep down weeds and reduce water evaporation from the soil, the maintenance is greatly reduced on places which are difficult to access.

In their traditional vertical guise, climbers are wonderful plants for improving the appearance of most houses and their surrounding walls and fences. Just a small selection of plants can provide year-round colour: swathes of evergreen, glossy-leaved, variegated ivy; clematis – some of which will be in flower virtually any month of the year; plus

EARLY SUMMER SCENT

Blue-mauve cascades of wisteria blossoms, with their coconut fragrance, herald the end of spring and the start of summer. Wisteria is best grown where the long racemes of flowers can hang down unhindered. (p.148)

jasmine and roses for scent. Clothed in flowers and foliage to soften and blur straight lines, a house and its boundaries will look attractive and welcoming.

Away from walls and fences, climbers can be trained over pergolas, arches and arbours to contribute enormously to the overall design of a garden. On a smaller scale, there are various free-standing frameworks which can be placed in a border to create instant height, or even on their own to make a focal point at, for example, the end of a path. In tubs, climbers make a handsome and unusual display, trained over frameworks that can vary from a simple home-made tripod of bamboo canes or a rustic wigwam of woven hazel or willow, to stylish obelisks crafted from timber or wrought iron. If you fancy a formal topiary feature without spending years clipping and training slow-growing box, there are tailor-made wire frames in many shapes and sizes that can be clothed with one of the many ivy cultivars in a relatively short space of time and kept in trim with shears or secateurs.

Established shrubs, conifers and trees make excellent supports for climbers, which can be threaded through their branches to give an extra garlanding of flowers. Where space is limited, doubling up plants in this fashion is just one way of introducing more colour into the garden. Take care with your choice of climber, though, or it could entwine the host plant (depending on its size and age) in a fatal grip. A small shrub such as the blue-flowered caryopteris would only be able to support an annual climber such as *Tropaeolum peregrinum*, Canary creeper, whereas a medium-sized, purple-leaved berberis could host a large-flowered clematis hybrid – white-flowered 'Marie Boisselot' would be an excellent choice. However, an old established tree could support a vigorous rambling rose like 'Seagull' with its single white blooms, or even a wisteria. When in doubt, plump for the less vigorous, well-behaved climbers such as sweet peas, large-flowered hybrid clematis and smaller-flowered species such as *Clematis viticella*.

One of the best places to see clematis festooning trees and shrubs is at Burford House Gardens, near Tenbury Wells in Worcestershire. Created over the past forty years by the late John Treasure and now in the care of Charles Chesshire, Burford House is home to the National Collection of *Clematis* and over two hundred species, hybrids and cultivars can be seen in the gardens. Truly, this is a place for inspiration on how to use clematis around the garden. See them partnered with mature shrubs, the colours carefully chosen for the best contrasts: deep ruby red 'Niobe' with a variegated dogwood; white 'Miss Bateman' with a purple-leaved *Cotinus*; and deep blue 'Ascotiensis' with the bright red climbing rose 'Parkdirektor Riggers'. With so many jewel-like flower colours to choose from, the possibilities are endless.

The growing habits of *Clematis viticella* are fully exploited too. This species and its many hybrids can be cut back almost to the ground in autumn or early spring. This tolerance is taken advantage of at Burford House Gardens where examples are trained over winter-flowering heathers to produce a mass of flowers from mid- to late summer. In autumn the clematis is cut back in time for the heathers to be seen in their full glory. Prostrate junipers are enlivened in the same way, and upright conifers are garlanded with unusual species such as pale yellow *C. rehderiana* (*C. veitchiana*) and white *C. montana* var. *sericea* (*C. chrysocoma* var. *sericea*).

For practical purposes, climbers are wonderful cover-all plants for concealing ugly walls, fences, pipes or other features. Drape rampant *Clematis montana* over an old oil tank, for example, or use instead evergreen ivy, a tolerant, handsome, and underrated plant. If occasional access is necessary for maintenance, there are fast-growing climbers that either die back in winter or will tolerate hard

VERSATILE GOLDEN CLIMBER

Golden-foliaged climbers are few and far between, so it is lucky that the golden-leaved hop, Humulus lupulus *'Aureus', is a tolerant, adaptable and fast-growing plant. It dies back to the ground in the autumn but regrows quickly in the spring. (p.148)*

pruning almost to the ground. Good examples include many ornamental peas – *Lathyrus* species, *Passiflora caerulea*, the blue passion flower, and ivory white *P. caerulea* 'Constance Elliott'. Another candidate is one of my all-time favourites – the golden hop, *Humulus lupulus* 'Aureus'. Female plants bear clusters of wonderfully aromatic flowers that can be harvested in autumn and encased in muslin to make a hop pillow, a traditional remedy for sleeplessness.

Annual climbers have a valuable part to play in the hanging garden, especially where some quick summer colour is required, and a trawl through a

HEDGE OF FLAME

A few sprigs of foliage peep out to show that there is a clipped yew hedge underneath this spectacular mass of Scotch flame flower, Tropaeolum speciosum. *With thin, scrambling stems, it is at its best growing over another plant. (p.148)*

few seed catalogues produces a fascinating selection of plants. The popular Canary creeper, *Tropaeolum peregrinum*, is a reliable and vigorous plant that can produce stems up to 4 metres (12 ft) long covered with bright yellow, prettily fringed flowers. There are many morning glories, including the old favourite *Ipomoea* (*Convolvulus*) *tricolor* 'Heavenly Blue', its huge flowers an almost unreal shade of sky blue. The blooms open in the morning and only last for one day, but they are produced in such profusion that one well-grown plant will often bear dozens of flowers each day. I go out every morning and count the number of flowers that have opened – my record to date is forty-two from one plant. Other, less usual annual climbers well worth looking out for include *Asarina* species or chickabiddy, *Cobaea scandens* and *Rhodochiton atrosanguineum*, the purple bell vine, with its unusually shaped, black-purple flowers.

Lovers of the less common have plenty of mouthwatering climbers to choose from. There are some on the borderline of frost-hardiness such as *Lapageria rosea*, popularly known as Chilean bell-flower, with its waxy, deep rose-pink trumpets; *Tropaeolum tuberosum* 'Ken Aslet' with spurred, orange-red, tubular flowers; and the bluebell creeper, *Sollya heterophylla* with delightful sky blue flowers. Those gardeners who are fortunate enough to have a conservatory have an even wider range of magnificent and exotic climbers to form living curtains, but that's another story altogether.

AUTUMN TAPESTRY

Left. *Choosing climbers with more than one season of interest makes the best use of wall space, especially if the garden is small. Autumn is a wonderful time for dazzling foliage colour, and the gleaming yellow leaves of the climbing hydrangea are second to none for cheering up a shady wall. A branch of Virginia creeper weaves through the gold, like a thread of colour running through a tapestry. (p.148)*

SUMMER FLOWERS FOR SHADE

Above. *In summer, the climbing hydrangea changes character completely, its fresh green foliage providing a cool back-cloth to the frothy heads of white flowers. This plant clings to the wall by means of lots of aerial roots, so there is no need for any special supports. This climber is slow to reach maturity, but your patience will be well rewarded. (p.148)*

'MADAME GALEN' REIGNS

Opposite. *The eye is immediately drawn to the vivid orange-red flowers of* Campsis *'Madame Galen', but tucked demurely under* the roof overhang is a basket of Parthenocissus tricuspidata *'Veitchii', or Boston ivy, with its overlapping leaves. (p.148)*

THE TURN OF THE VINE

Above. *In autumn, the tables will be turned when the foliage of* Parthenocissus *takes on fiery shades of red. Here the older leaves of this* close relative of the Boston ivy have already turned colour. But soon the whole plant will appear to be on fire. (p.148)*

ONE-YEAR WONDERS

Opposite. *Annual climbers are perfect for clothing newly erected arches and supports. This unusual plant is* Ipomoea quamoclit *which bears tubular flowers that are first red, fading to orange and finally to creamy yellow — so each stem holds a mixture of colours. (p.148)*

BOLD FOLIAGE BASKET

Above. *An unusual wooden basket has been planted with* Vitis coignetiae. *In autumn the large leaves will develop wonderful tints of red and orange. Enough of a breeze comes through this sheltered spot to stir the black wind chimes into delicate voice. (p.148)*

FLOWERS FOR FRAGRANT POSIES

Opposite. Sweet peas, favourites with gardeners for many years, are easy to grow from seed. A few plants trained up elegant obelisks or, more modestly, wigwams of canes, can provide pillars of fragrance and ensure there are always plenty of blooms for picking. (p.149)

VERSATILE VITICELLA

Above. If I had to choose my favourite group of clematis, the viticellas would win every time. They bear masses of small flowers from mid-summer onwards and are ideal for growing through other plants as well as up supports, such as this stylish timber obelisk. (p.149)

CLEMATIS-CLAD BALUSTRADE

Opposite. *Low boundaries are often left bare, so it is pleasing to see this one dressed with a handsome* clematis. *Its colour harmonizes well with the double-flowered busy lizzies. (p.149)*

CLEMATIS BALLS

Above. *Will Tooby at Bransford Garden Plants loves experimenting: these clematis 'balls' have been* created by wiring two hanging baskets together. These hybrids are well suited to containers . (p.149)

FRONT DOOR FESTOONED

Opposite. *Climbers on the front of a house give warmth and friendliness of character that could otherwise be lacking. One of the most rampant species, this* Clematis montana *has long since outgrown the trellis to the left of the door. It must suffer a stern pruning after flowering every year to keep it from spreading further and turning the house into an impenetrable Sleeping Beauty's palace. But at present this reliable climber confines itself to a confetti-like scattering of petals on the shoulders of people going in and out. (p.149)*

A SPECTACULAR SPRING GARDEN

Above. *Spring: when the day begins to draw out and the garden fills with blossom and birdsong. After the bare bones of the garden's structure have stood out bleakly all winter it is wonderful to see them gradually become covered with fresh flowers and foliage. With ample room to tumble casually along the weathered brick wall, the deep pink of* Clematis montana *'Tetrarose' is echoed in the paler blooms of the flowering cherry. Against the house wall, a gnarled old wisteria is opening the first of its fragrant blue flowers. In the clear evening air, it is easy to imagine a blackbird perched on the topmost branch of the cherry tree, singing his melodious spring song. (p.149)*

PINK PERFECTION

Opposite. *A large urn is roomy
enough for two: for spring there is*
Clematis montana *var. rubens,
and for summer* C. *'Comtesse de
Bouchard' forms a loose mound of
pale pink flowers.* (p.149)

BLUE MOOD

Above. *The blue bronze tones of
the stoneware urn enhance the
flowers of* Clematis *'Elsa Späth'.
The pot is tucked in a shady corner
as hybrid clematis hate having hot
'feet'.* (p.149)

GOLDEN LANTERNS

Latest and loveliest of the clematis to flower is C. tangutica. *The dazzling golden lanterns mingle with the fluffy seedheads of the earlier blooms against a background of sea-green foliage. Entangled with the clematis is* Eccremocarpus scaber *which blooms from mid-summer onwards, producing clusters of orange-yellow flowers.* Eccremocarpus *often dies back to the ground in winter and hard frosts usually kill it, but this is little problem as plants can easily be raised from seed in spring to flower later the same year.* (p.149)

OVERGROWN GATEWAY

Opposite. *Perennial peas can be left to run wild as they die back to ground-level each winter. This is* Lathyrus rotundifolius, *the Persian pea, growing in the gardens of Burford House. (p.149)*

PAINTED FOLIAGE

Above. *Against a shower of golden laburnum, it looks for all the world as though this mischievous sprite has* been at work with a paint brush, *splashing these* Actinidia kolomikta *leaves with bright pink. (p.149)*

ELEGANT FOLIAGE, COOL CONTRASTS
Ferns and grasses

lthough ferns and ornamental grasses have been creeping into garden fashion in a small way, they tend to be greatly underused when it comes to containers. Yet their qualities are subtle and enduring, with an almost endless variation of leaf shape and plant forms coloured in delicate shades of green, often touched with white or gold. Inevitably, such low-key plants have tended to be overshadowed by jazzy, attention-grabbing flowers, but there comes a time when the eye longs to rest on something more soothing to relieve the constant pageant of bright blooms. Not only does the foliage interest of ferns and grasses last from spring to autumn, and in some cases all year round, but many are perennial and also hardy. What more could any gardener ask?

Where ferns and grasses really come into their own is in shady situations. Nearly every house has a dark corner outside, often prominent, such as by a doorway, and the majority of small town gardens are inevitably lacking in sunshine. Hanging baskets and containers filled with these leafy plants are particularly in keeping with such sites. There are many grasses that do well in partial shade, and all ferns thrive without any sunlight.

LEAVES IN CONTRAST

The large-leaved hosta takes prominence now this basket – seen hanging up on page 55 – is resting on a bench. The slender blades of the variegated greater pond sedge rub shoulders with the ornamental vine. (p.149)

If you fancy a few flowers to nestle among the foliage, add some shade-loving bedding plants like busy lizzies or fuchsias, both of which come in an enormous range of flower colours. Although colour choice is very much down to personal preference, I would recommend the paler pastel shades rather than garish colours, which tend to look rather out of place in a shady spot. I often prefer to opt for white flowers, because the blooms seem to reflect every last bit of light and they become almost luminous in the twilight. There are ornamental grasses for both sun and shade. If your only encounter with these plants has been the ubiquitous pampas grass, look again. Recent years have seen the introduction of many attractive grasses, mainly with colourful foliage and a compact habit that makes them ideal for baskets and other containers. Their elegant yet bold shapes make them perfect for planting alone or taking a central position in a basket to be a dramatic foil to flowering plants.

Among the smallest grasses are the festucas, which form neat little hedgehog-like mounds, good for edging. They vary in colour from the intense blue of *Festuca glauca* – 'Elijah Blue' has the deepest colouring – to the fresh green of *F. gautieri* (*F. scoparia*) and greeny gold of *F.* 'Golden Toupee'. The grass-like sedges include some handsome plants such as *Carex hachijoensis* 'Evergold' (*C. oshimensis* 'Evergold') with narrow green-and-gold striped leaves, *C. siderosticha* 'Variegata' whose wide green leaves are edged with white, and to contrast, *C. comans* Bronze Form with fine bronze-red leaves.

Slightly larger grasses with a graceful, arching habit include *Hakonechloa macra* 'Aureola' with gorgeous gold-and-green striped leaves. *Koeleria glauca*, the crested hair grass, has glaucous foliage as does *Leymus arenarius*. The latter is best planted in a container by itself as it can be invasive. For a sunny site, the fountain grasses, *Pennisetum*, are superb from mid-summer onwards when they bear masses of flower heads which look exactly like huge, hairy caterpillars! The most compact species for containers is *P. orientale*.

Although nearly all grasses die back in autumn, I prefer to leave the dead foliage standing until late winter before cutting it back, prior to the new season's growth appearing. The foliage of many species becomes bleached a beautiful parchment colour in autumn, and on chilly winter mornings each arching blade becomes silvered with frost to make an enchanting picture.

Some grasses and sedges, however, are evergreen, notably *Carex oshimensis* 'Variegata' and *C. hachijoensis* 'Evergold', and I like to use them for foliage colour in winter window-boxes and hanging baskets. Another of my favourites for this purpose is the black-leaved lily grass, *Ophiopogon planiscapus* 'Nigrescens', with its midnight black foliage and clusters of shiny black berries in winter. A surprising number of ferns are evergreen, including the hart's tongue fern and many *Polypodium* and *Polystichum* species; this is an important point to bear in mind when selecting plants for a year-round, high-profile position.

One look at a collection of ferns makes me realize the word 'green' is totally inadequate to describe the enormous range of different shades. The heyday of ferns was over a hundred years ago, when the Victorians had a short-lived but intense mania for collecting every possible variation. Wild populations were plundered and many ferns were dug up and sold. Any unusual ones were immediately seized by collectors for their private ferneries. Some of the more spectacular foliage variations bordered on the bizarre, with leaves that were contorted, crested or frilled. The naming of such variants was equally complicated, for example *Polystichum angulare divisilobum plumosum densum erectum*!

Today such plundering of native habitats is as unacceptable as the killing of endangered birds and animals for collections – also a popular practice with many Victorians. The choice of ferns now available is also far narrower. Indeed, you will be lucky to find more than half a dozen different species on sale in most garden centres, though specialist nurseries offer a much more rewarding selection. It is obviously down to personal taste whether you prefer those with more ornate leaf forms or the simpler lines of the species. I confess a preference for the latter as I think they look more effective in a mixed display.

Ferns are ideal for a hanging garden as they adapt well to baskets, wall pots and troughs which can be used to bring life to the gloomiest, darkest spots. Other potential sites which are often overlooked are the niches and crevices in a wall, the danker the better, which can be planted with ferns. *Asplenium scolopendrium*, the hart's tongue fern, and *Polypodium vulgare*, the common polypody, are more tolerant of drought than other ferns, and they will often self-seed over a wall so it becomes sprinkled with soft points of foliage. In fact, grasses and ferns in containers and on walls need little maintenance. Apart from cutting back dead foliage each winter and top-dressing with a little fresh compost and fertilizer each spring (see page 140), they can be left undisturbed for several years. Once the clump has become large and congested, it can be divided into several pieces in spring and replanted in much the same way as perennials.

The world of ferns and grasses is a fascinating one, and when I was first seduced by their charms many years ago, a patch of the garden untouched by sunlight became an asset rather than a liability. What were once shady, dull and lifeless corners have been transformed by wall pots and baskets, overflowing with wonderful arching foliage.

BLUE AND GOLD GRASSES

Tall slender flowerheads rise above the blue-green leaves of Leymus arenarius, *a superb contrast to Bowles' golden sedge. Genuinely old chimney pots are now in short supply, so it is pleasing to see there are some good modern terracotta 'chimney' pots available. (p.150)*

ABOVE THE ORDINARY

These two common plants are elevated from the ranks of the ordinary by putting them in a wall trough. The ornamental deadnettle is a vigorous plant which can, quite frankly, be a nuisance in the border but here it forms delicate trails of foliage that reach to the ground. Though the long stems die back in winter, the younger growth stays green right through the year, as do the glossy fronds of the hart's tongue fern. I chose these plants for a dark, shady spot outside my back door in order to have some long-lasting and trouble-free foliage to greet me, and they do the job admirably. (p.150)

WATERFALL OF GOLD

Opposite. *With its bright foliage and an elegant, cascading habit, this golden-leaved* Hakonechloa *grass is my especial favourite. The trouble is, it needs to be raised up high as my cat loves to run the leaves through her teeth, nipping off the dainty tips! (p.150)*

LONG-LASTING LEAVES

Above. *Under my shady kitchen window, the spiky black leaves of* Ophiopogon *peep out of the top of this long wall trough in strong contrast to the central* Hosta *'June'. In front, multi-coloured* Ajuga *leaves begin to mingle with plants at a lower level. (p.150)*

HAIRY HEAD

Sedges form elegant, arching clumps of grass-like foliage that are nearly all ideal for container plantings. Sprouting out of this head of David is Carex conica *'Snowline', its leaves delicately striped with green and white. Such a planting adds a touch of humour to the garden, even more so if the aptly named* Festuca *'Golden Toupee' were to be used instead – though I must say the stone-faced chap does not look at all happy about the idea! (p.150)*

HEARTY HALF-HARDIES
Frost-tender perennials

With so many plants already at our disposal, it is rare indeed nowadays for a new group of plants to take the gardening world by storm. But this is exactly what has happened with frost-tender perennials which came to prominence on the gardening scene just a few years ago, and which are fast revolutionizing the look of hanging baskets and containers. Because they are relatively new to most gardeners, I decided to look at them separately from old favourites such as pelargoniums and fuchsias which have been treated traditionally as annual bedding plants, although they too are frost-tender perennials.

The majority of tender perennials trail to a greater or lesser extent and so are perfectly suited to a hanging garden. A number of plants like diascias, gazanias and osteospermums form spreading masses of flowers and foliage that tip gently over the sides of a container. But there are some really magnificent trailers which are spectacular for hanging baskets, forming cascading curtains of stems. A few of the best include *Lobelia richardii*, with clear blue flowers, which is a wonderful perennial relative of the well-known bedding favourite, *Lobelia erinus*. Nothing beats *Bidens ferulifolia* for sheer mass production of small, bright golden flowers. It contrasts beautifully with the deep blue, fan-shaped flowers

VEGETABLE RACK IN HIDING

With so many different colours and flower shapes, tender perennials make an incomparable show through the summer. This splendid cascade, created by Della Connolly, is planted in an old vegetable rack. (p.150)

of scaevola. In a really sun-baked spot, you may manage to persuade *Lotus bertholetii* and *L. maculatus*, often shy to flower, to produce their red or orange 'claws'. However, they are more than worth growing for their long trails clad in needle-like, grey-green leaves.

I must confess to having a particularly soft spot for tender perennials. Some years ago I fell in love at first sight with *Mimulus aurantiacus*, a shrubby musk with gorgeous peachy apricot flowers. I paid an exorbitant price for a plant as, at the time, they were few and far between. But the money was well-spent. Since then, although I have added dozens of other plants to my collection of tender perennials, the mimulus still takes first place in my affections. (It can be seen in the bottom left-hand corner of the picture on page 111.)

I am immensely pleased to see so many of these plants reaching a wider audience, and I feel these summer-flowering stunners really are the plants that will hold centre stage in the future. Not only do their flower colours cover just about the whole spectrum, but the shapes of the actual blooms are enormously varied. Even better, the plants themselves have attractive forms and handsome foliage. Because large plants can be bought in or overwintered, they can add maturity to any display within a very short time of planting.

Just about all tender perennials are sun-lovers that prefer a well-drained site. A look at their origins is enough to see why they really excel themselves in hot, dry summers. Plants belonging to the genera *Bidens*, *Mimulus* and *Penstemon* come from the southern and western United States; *Felicia*,

Gazania, *Helichrysum* and *Osteospermum* originate from South and West Africa; and *Verbena* comes from southern South America. With such sun-baked origins, these plants give an unrivalled performance in summer containers for hot, south-facing sites in particular. Where other seasonal plants look a bit hot and bothered, these tender perennials lap up the heat, producing bigger and better explosions of flowers as the summer goes on.

In order to show some of the newest and best plants, I turned to several different professional growers and gardeners, including two wholesale plant producers who specialize in frost-tender perennials. Surrey nurseryman Peter Higgs is an avid enthusiast of these versatile plants. He began growing them in the early 1980s, starting with helichrysums and verbenas, and the range expanded rapidly. Within a few years the nursery was marketing them as 'patio plants' for containers, and demand just kept growing. Now the range is impressive and continually expanding to take in new varieties of *Diascia*, *Lobelia*, *Brachyscome*, *Sutera* and *Verbena*. The old, wooden-framed greenhouses are a veritable treasure-trove of new plants under trial or being 'bulked up' to reach saleable numbers. Many of these new plants reach the nursery through Peter's network of fellow enthusiasts in Britain and abroad, who swap plants and compare notes.

New plants are put through their paces on the nursery for about three years before they ever reach the gardening public. On a large paved area, built in part to resemble a patio, plants are grown 'with a suitable amount of neglect', as Peter describes it, to see how they perform in a typical garden situation. Only when they grow to a satisfactory standard are they produced in quantity and sold to retail nurseries.

Peter loves experimenting with new plants, and he feels very strongly that gardeners should be encouraged to do the same: 'Nowadays there is

PINK AND WHITE PERFECTION

A clump of double-flowered busy lizzies tops a billowing mass of variegated Plectranthus, *a useful plant for foliage interest. The pale colours show up beautifully against the dark hedge of Leyland cypress. (p.150)*

almost too much in the way of instruction and too much emphasis on doing everything the "right way", and I think it can make people afraid of plants. In fact, you can get away with most things when you're gardening, the important point is not to be afraid of trying something different. After all, plants are such lovely things – they make me feel very humble for we cannot create anything more beautiful.'

Down in the Vale of Evesham, Proculture Plants represents the high-tech side of horticulture. Most plants here are raised by micropropagation or tissue culture, by which a tiny bud tip is grown in a test-tube in a laboratory environment. Once a small plantlet has developed from the bud, it is acclimatized to the outside world and grown on in soil. The advantage of raising plants by this method is speed. When a new plant appears on the scene, it can take quite a few years to produce enough plants from cuttings to satisfy a widespread market. But because only a comparatively small amount of plant tissue is needed for micropropagation, this method allows dozens or even hundreds of new plants to be raised from just one parent plant.

Professional gardeners and designers are increasingly using tender perennials to create outstanding summer displays; among them Della Connolly, head gardener at the Red Cross headquarters in Surrey and Rupert Golby, garden designer and author of *The Container Gardener*. Now these plants are widely available from retail outlets so ordinary gardeners can also use them to the full.

There are plenty of up-and-coming tender perennials on the market to maintain novelty in the hanging garden. Here are just some which have caught my eye recently. *Alonsoa warscewiczii* 'Peachy-Keen' and *A. warscewiczii* have long, slender, trailing stems covered with masses of small flowers, in peach and red respectively. Look out too for buff and white variants of *Mimulus aurantiacus*, palest pink *Nemesia* 'Confetti' and dark lavender blue *Nemesia umbonata* 'Woodcote', as well as numerous new gazanias and osteospermums. The trouble is, they are all so tempting that I always end up with far more plants than I have room for!

WIRE TRAYS ON STONE

Opposite. *The stone pedestal suggests an impressive container; but in fact the plants grow in two wire trays, one on top of the other. Della* *Connolly works on the theory that if enough plants are used, the appearance of the container is immaterial and it certainly works. (p.151)*

FOLIAGE MEDLEY

Above. *Foliage plants such as* Plectranthus, Tolmiea *and golden* Lamium, *planted in a jardinière, stand out superbly against a huge* *cascade of purple Surfinia petunias. Free-standing containers can be easily moved around to ring the changes. (p.151)*

EMPTY CENTREPIECE

Opposite. When grouping many different plants together, it is easy to get carried away and throw in all colours. By restricting this scheme to *white, yellow and pink, the overall effect is harmonious. However, it is the large, empty pot that catches the eye in this display. (p.151)*

LONG-FLOWERING DIASCIAS

Above. Diascias are another of my favourite plants, with a seemingly endless supply of deep pink flowers. But it is possible to have too much of *a good thing, and the silvery green helichrysum foliage in the middle breaks up what could otherwise be an overpowering planting. (p.151)*

BIDENS TUMBLING DOWN

Opposite. *The plantings on these pages are both by Rupert Golby. They have similar pots and an identical background, but the moods they create are very different. The gleaming yellow flowers of* bidens *dominate a cheerful display with* an abundance of daisies borne on long, sprawling stems: it is one of my favourite plants for raised containers. However, it is worth pinching out the tips from time to time to stop the plant from becoming too straggly. (p.152)

MUD WALL BACKDROP

Above. *In total contrast is the soft, almost sombre, combination of* Verbena 'Aphrodite' *and the silvery scandent shoots of* Plecostachys serpyllifolia. *Photographed at Whichford Pottery, the unusual background is a mud wall, one of* several constructed by Jim Keeling and made with a mixture of waste clay, sand, straw and a little lime, capped with a tile roof. Within their bounds two small and secluded gardens have been created next to the pottery. (p.152)

CHIMNEY POT AT HOME

Opposite. *The deep, rich pink flowers of diascia tumble down the sides of a lichen covered, weathered chimney pot, harmonizing wonderfully with the crushed blackberry colour of the paintwork. As a chimney pot is, in effect, part of a house, it also looks perfectly at home against the brickwork. Unfortunately, old chimney pots tend to be expensive since they have become popular with gardeners, so it is worth snapping up any reasonably priced ones. (p.152)*

SPECTACULAR SUMMER COLLECTION

Above. *A magnificent collection of Peter Higgs' tender perennials that includes some of his newest and most exceptional plants. The most eye-catching is* Verbena *'Pink Parfait', on the left, with its huge heads of candy pink flowers, far larger than those of other verbenas. White flowers dominate the centre of the display topped by the upright stems of* Nemesia *'Innocence'. From this the cascading stems of* Sutera cordata *'Snowflake' seem to flow down, making a perfect foil for the brighter colours and larger flowers of the other plants. (p.152)*

SURFINIA PETUNIA CASCADE

Opposite. *Unsurpassed for vigour and sheer mass production of flowers, it is hardly surprising that Surfinia petunias have shot to fame in a very short space of time. Bred in Japan, a hybrid between seed-raised and species petunias, these* *vigorous plants are best planted in a tall or suspended container by themselves. This fine example is 'Purple Mini', bearing masses of vibrant purple flowers. Other colours available include white, lilac-pink and bright pink. (p.153)*

HANGING BASKET TREE

Above. *Even when there is nowhere to put up brackets for baskets, it is still possible to have a first class floral display by using one of these ingenious, free standing, hanging-basket stands made of wrought iron. The baskets, created by Proculture Plants, contain some* *exceptional trailing plants. On the right-hand side, double-flowered red busy lizzies mingle with the perennial nasturtium 'Red Wonder' and the rather unusual 'poker' flowers of* Acalypha. *The left-hand basket is a mass of blue-mauve* scaevola. (p.152)

FLORAL NICHE

Opposite. *A stone urn spills over with flowers and foliage. The large, palmate leaves belong to the castor* oil plant Ricinus communis, *which can be grown from seed and treated as an annual. (p.153)*

HOUSE-PLANT HANGING BASKET

Above. *Most of these plants are more commonly seen indoors rather than outside. A range of foliage plants with contrasting shapes and colours has been used to create an unusual hanging basket display.*

Spiky leaved spider plants, variegated ivy, a weeping fig, and the pick-a-back plant, Tolmiea, *contrast with the purple leaves and slender, dangling stems of* Saxifraga stolonifera. *(p.153)*

SMALL-SCALE VERSATILITY
Perennials, alpines and shrubs

way from the blazing flowers, so typical of summer baskets, there is a whole world of trailing perennial plants to explore. Shrubs, herbaceous perennials and heathers have always been looked upon as plants for the border, but once they cease to be viewed solely for this purpose, there is no end to the variety of permanent plants that can be used for hanging gardens. Unlike the majority of summer-flowering annuals and frost-tender perennials, many of these permanent plants tolerate partial or even total shade, so they are particularly valuable for cheering up a dingy corner.

My main criterion in selecting plants for containers is that they should be reasonably attractive over a long period, not some two-week wonder that looks dazzlingly lovely in flower but dull before and after. So the foliage must be reasonably appealing in colour or shape – preferably both – and the overall habit must also be fairly good for it to occupy a high-profile position.

Plants with long-lasting foliage interest include ornamental deadnettles, like *Lamium maculatum* 'Beacon Silver' with silvery white leaves and pink flowers. The foliage of *L. maculatum* 'White Nancy' is similar but the flowers are white. *L. maculatum* 'Aureum' is best planted away from strong sunlight which can scorch its bright golden leaves.

TUMBLING DOWNHILL

Alpines and perennials are ideal for sloping sites, where they can tumble downhill to form loose cushions of flowers and foliage. In early summer alpines are at their most colourful. (p.153)

Ornamental brambles naturally trail and sprawl. *Rubus pentalobus* (*R. calycinoides*) and *R. tricolor* have handsome evergreen foliage, as do the periwinkles, *Vinca*. Several periwinkles have variegated foliage as well as blue or white spring flowers – the blue flowers of *Vinca minor* 'Argenteovariegata' look especially good against the green-and-white leaves.

The over-zealous propensities of certain plants make them ideal subjects for suspended containers. Indeed, solitary confinement in a pot is the only way I allow some plants into my garden, as once in the border they set out to take over the whole patch with single-minded intensity. In particular, I am thinking of ground-cover plants like the variegated deadnettle – *Lamium galeobdolen* 'Florentinum' (see page 72), the greater periwinkle – *Vinca major* and the wall harebell – *Campanula portenschlagiana*. Being evergreen they will last up to five years in a basket provided they are fed and watered regularly and repotted or top-dressed every spring.

As a useful pointer to many different trailing plants, look for the catch-all description of 'ground-cover'. After all, if a plant carpets the ground, the chances are it will also hang down in a curtain over the edge of a container. Gardeners use such plants all the time in borders, and perhaps their very ordinariness has resulted in them being overlooked for containers. But use them in tall pots, wall troughs, or hanging baskets, and you will find that they become a real talking point. Even the most common plant can be used in a way to make it really stand out from the crowd, such as one planting that sadly did not mature in time to be photographed for this book. It was an arrangement of three flower pots, placed one on top of the other – the smallest on the top, like the tiers of a wedding cake, and planted solely with variegated periwinkles that cascaded down from one pot to the next. In time the natural layering habit of the plant would ensure that many of the shoots would take root to create a luxuriant mass of foliage.

The term 'alpine' is, like ground cover, a blanket description for the many dwarf perennials suitable for rock gardens. They vary from exquisite miniatures that only grow a few centimetres (an inch or so) wide to vigorous plants that can reach as much as a metre (3 feet 3 inches) across. It is these more rampant plants that are of interest for a hanging garden. They include *Persicaria* (*Polygonum*) *vaccinifolium*, a dwarf knotweed with pretty pale pink poker-like flower heads, and old favourites such as aubrieta, arabis, *Aurinia saxatilis* (*Alyssum saxatile*), pinks (*Dianthus*) and alpine phlox. For a really sunny site, choose sun or rock roses – *Helianthemum*, *Hypericum olympicum* and *Euphorbia myrsinites*. As well as being ideal for larger rock gardens, these plants are also excellent tumbling in loose cushions down a steep bank or spilling over the edge of large tubs and raised beds.

There are a few more compact gems for containers which can be found by searching among the herbaceous perennials. Those with a neat habit and attractive foliage are excellent for the centre of a container or a wall trough. My favourites include *Heuchera micrantha* 'Palace Purple', and 'Pewter Moon' with its silver-mottled purple leaves; I prefer to cut off the spikes of insignificant white flowers so the leaves continue to hold centre stage. The smaller hostas such as 'Halcyon' or 'June' have bold, attractive leaves and, for a mixture of flower and foliage interest, look out for *Pyrethropsis* (*Chrysanthemum*) *hosmariense* with its silver filigree foliage. The white daisies are produced over an astonishingly long period, and I have even seen it flowering in the middle of winter.

There are a few miscellaneous plants worthy of mention. The multi-coloured *Houttuynia cordata*, variously listed as 'Chameleon', 'Tricolor' or 'Harlequin', is often sold as a pond plant though it thrives in any soil that is not allowed to dry out. It has a vigorous, suckering habit for which reason I prefer to plant it on its own. The dainty leaved mind-your-own-business or baby's tears (*Soleirolia soleirolii*) is wonderful for greening up a damp, shady spot, either planted in pots or allowed to run along wall crevices or risers between steps. But, I must add a word of warning: it can make an absolute pest of itself in mild areas if it escapes into the border or the lawn as it can be hard to eradicate.

Heathers are excellent for winter as well as summer flowers, and they are ideal for lots of different places, including hanging baskets. The summer-flowering callunas are perhaps less valuable for containers as there is no shortage of flowering plants to choose from at that time of year, but *Erica carnea* cultivars are really useful as they flower from the middle of winter through to spring. The flowers come in different shades of pink and red, with a few white-flowered cultivars such as 'Whitehall' and 'Springwood White'. There are some with golden foliage, too; 'Foxhollow' and 'Westwood Yellow' are both suitable for baskets. Try combining a few white heathers with pink-flowered cultivars such as 'Winter Beauty' or 'Springwood Pink'. Add some blue, winter-flowering pansies, a variegated ivy and some cream or yellow crocuses, and you will have a hanging basket full of cheerful colour through the gloomiest months of the year.

All the plants I have mentioned so far should give a good display within a short time, and for several years provided they are top-dressed each spring with fresh compost and slow-release fertilizer (see page 140). Whether you prefer plants for short- or long-term effect, it is well worth trying some of these 'hanging' perennials or smaller scandant shrubs. Most will look good for a long period but, during their 'off' months the containers can be moved out of sight to make way for an in-season display. Yet another bonus of hanging baskets.

HIGH-RISE HOUSELEEK

The fleshy rosettes of this little sempervivum, or houseleek, have filled a small Whichford wall pot and spilled over the sides. A topping of coarse grit prevents the fleshy stems from becoming waterlogged. (p.153)

SPRING GOLD-DUST

Opposite. *The flowers of the gold-dust flower,* Aurinia saxatilis, *also known as* Alyssum saxatile, *are startlingly bright after the gloom of winter. This plant is ideal for covering a sunny rock wall or the front of a raised bed, or anywhere with well-drained soil. (p.153)*

SOFTER SHADES

Above. *Altogether softer and more subtle in colour is the dainty trailing Gypsophila repens 'Rosea', never happier than when it can hang its slender stems down a wall or over rock-work. The pale lilac flowers are perfectly complemented by the soft green, arching fronds of a fern, which has self-seeded to pop up in the middle of the clump. (p.153)*

SOFTENING A STAIRWAY

Opposite. *How stark these steps would look without this erigeron and lady's mantle. Some gardeners detest such rampant plants but I love their billowing effects. (p.154)*

LATE FLOWERS AND AUTUMN FOLIAGE

Above. *Towards the end of summer, the shrubby plumbago opens its clusters of clear blue flowers. The leaves will shortly develop deep red tints. (p.154)*

COOLING INFLUENCE

Opposite. *A sheet of starch white candytuft is a beautiful sight in spring. It can be used to 'cool down' some of the hotter colours that tend to predominate in the rock garden at this time of year. (p.154)*

PLANT-FILLED WALL

Above. *Dry-stone walls can play host to a first-class selection of plants, which thrive in seemingly impossibly small pockets of soil in the cracks. Sage green, dimpled leaves of* Geranium renardii *mingle with a cushion of campanula, and the dainty flowers and leaves of* Corydalis ochroleuca *shelter underneath. (p.154)*

FACE AT THE WINDOW

Left. *People either love this head peeping out of the foliage, or they find it creepy as I do! The plants are mostly evergreen, so this window-box maintains its interest from autumn through to spring, with curtains of ivy, blue juniper, and* Gaultheria procumbens *with bright red berries. (p.154)*

EARLY SUMMER MEDLEY

Above. *Perennials and frost-tender plants join forces for early summer colour. Variegated ivies and grasses arch and trail and, together with hostas, their strongly shaped and variegated foliage provides an outstanding backdrop for the blue and yellow flowers of felicia, bidens and velvety flowered pansies. (p.154)*

A COOK'S DELIGHT
Vegetables, fruit and herbs

here are few experiences in gardening to rival the deep-down satisfaction of watching your own fruit and vegetables reach maturity, then eating them with delight. And edible plants have their place in the hanging garden so you can enjoy the taste of strawberries picked fresh and eaten still warm from the sun, the crispness of just-harvested lettuce, or the flavour imparted by a sprinkling of fresh herbs.

Through the centuries, business rather than pleasure has ruled the kitchen garden and kept it hidden away behind walls or hedges wherever possible. The most notable historical exception was in France during the seventeenth and eighteenth centuries when potagers became all the rage. The trend for growing vegetables and herbs within 'knots', or low hedges, began at Versailles in the late seventeenth century with the construction of the *grand potager du roi*. This became a model for ornamental potagers on the estates of the wealthy and influential throughout the country.

Fortunately for today's small-space gardeners, vegetables and fruit have shed their lowly image and are now an integral part of many an ornamental garden. It is not unusual to see decorative plantings of fruit and vegetables, and sometimes even entire gardens of edible plants, with nasturtiums and the

various cucurbits trained over arches and tripods. One of the best permanent British potager-style gardens can be seen at Barnsley House in Gloucestershire, the home of garden designer and writer Rosemary Verey.

Correspondingly, the seed breeders have been working hard to produce varieties that look as good as they taste. Browse through almost any seed catalogue and you will find such things as golden-fruited courgettes, purple-podded French beans, striped tomatoes, and a host of attractive salad crops. Alongside them is a new generation of mini-vegetables which are ideal for raising in containers, as they have been selected because they can be grown closely together and harvested whilst young and succulent. These are not plants to be tucked out of sight behind a high wall. Today's vegetables demand a prime position in containers.

Growing edible plants in containers has several great advantages over raising them in the ground, and convenience often comes top of the list. On a wet night when I am cooking dinner, I would much rather take a few steps outside the door for a bay leaf or reach up to a handy basket for a sprig of parsley, than grope my way down the garden in the dark. I can assure anyone that the experience of treading on a large slug in bare feet is not one to be repeated!

On the subject of slugs, and snails too, these pests seem more reluctant to crawl up the sides of a pot, so their favourite plants like runner beans and lettuces have a greater chance of survival. Any pests that do make the ascent can be caught by putting a band of non-setting glue or petroleum jelly around the pot's rim. Last, but certainly not least, of the

TASTY BASKET

Today's vegetables look as good as they taste. Loose-leaf lettuce, so-called because you can pick a few leaves at a time rather than the whole plant, is perfect for hanging baskets and comes in several colours. (p.154)

advantages is that growing vegetables and herbs in containers is often the only solution for the increasing number of small garden owners. With so many attractive plants available, there is no need to sacrifice anything in the way of visual appeal.

Climbing vegetables are especially suitable for tiny gardens as they make maximum use of the available space. Runner beans are worth growing for their attractive flowers alone; indeed, when they were first introduced to Britain a couple of hundred years ago, they were treated purely as ornamental plants for many years. Easy to grow from seed, they can be trained up a tripod of canes, up a trellis or over an arch or pergola. To help attract pollinating insects to the bean flowers, try growing some sweet peas alongside. The flowers look delightful together, and you will have the added bonus of the delicious sweet-pea fragrance. A relative of the runner bean, and even more ornamental, is a new variant of the lablab bean, or *Lablab purpureus* (*Dolichos lablab*), called 'Ruby Moon'. Bronze-green foliage provides a handsome backdrop for the mauve flowers, which are followed by velvety purple flat pods that turn dark green when cooked.

Marrows, courgettes and squashes can either be left to trail from large containers, or the more vigorous can be trained upwards over a support. All the fruits look attractive but some are more colourful than others, such as those of the bright yellow courgette 'Gold Rush'. These fruits look particularly good on the dinner table, sliced thinly in salads or in thicker chunks to serve with dips. The pale, creamy white squashes 'Tivoli' and 'Butternut' can be cooked whole to make a handsome side dish to a roast dinner. Large marrows make a main course in themselves, stuffed with a red kidney bean mixture and served with a cheese sauce. The plants mentioned so far are deep-rooting with big appetites. They need large containers and a compost high in organic matter. However, for smaller containers such as hanging baskets and window-boxes, there are plenty of salad vegetables with shallow roots. The prettiest loose-leaf lettuces include 'Lollo Rosso' and 'Raisa'. Their frilled, reddish leaves look lovely against the pale green foliage of 'Lollo Bionda'. Other leaf vegetables worth trying are claytonia or winter purslane, corn salad or lamb's lettuce, land cress, and rocket which has a strong, spicy taste.

Most herbs are ideal for growing in containers, with benefits that reach way beyond our taste buds. For thousands of years they have been used to cure all manner of ills, and today more and more people are turning to herbal remedies for minor ailments. Among my favourite medicinal plants is sage, a natural antiseptic, which I take as sage tea to sooth a sore throat. I grow *Salvia officinalis* 'Icterina' in a large trough close by my back door, its greyish gold foliage spilling over the sides most attractively. The sage combines well with another, to me, indispensable herb – chamomile whose flowers can be infused to make a relaxing drink for the late evening. Other good herbs for hanging baskets include golden marjoram, parsley, pennyroyal, and thymes – especially those with coloured foliage like *Thymus* × *citriodorus* 'Archer's Gold' and 'Doone Valley'.

As with vegetables, comparatively few of us have enough space for an old-fashioned fruit garden, but it is possible to have a delicious, if modest, harvest from a hanging garden. Strawberries can be grown to trail down the sides of tall containers or special strawberry pots. Fruiting briars such as blackberries, loganberries and tayberries, and raspberry canes are better grown in the ground. All these climbers can be trained to clad walls, fences, pergolas or arches. They can also be tied into a post-and-wire framework along the garden boundary – if you trust your neighbours not to scrump the fruit – or used as a dividing screen within the garden itself. Most briar fruits have canes covered in vicious thorns, so if you often have to walk close to the plant it would be wise to opt for a thornless variety. Look out for blackberries such as 'Merton Thornless' and 'Oregon Thornless', and the unimaginatively named Loganberry 'LY 654'.

If you have been used to relegating fruit and vegetables to an out-of-the-way part of the garden, it may take a little while to get used to edible plants rubbing shoulders with petunias and pelargoniums. But there really is nothing better than enjoying the fruits of your labours be it a succulent strawberry or a juicy tomato.

FLOWERS FOR SPICY SALADS

Flowers can be edible too. Vivid nasturtium flowers make a gorgeously colourful salad garnish, and the peppery taste of the leaves can add a zing to salads. The plants look wonderful in all sorts of garden situations. Here in combination with a courgette plant they tumble in a colourful mass out of an unusual pumpkin-shaped pot, eventually to cover the front of the raised bed. (p.154)

COLOUR CO-ORDINATED VEGETABLES

Opposite. *Vegetables can be combined to create an intriguing combination of foliage colour and texture. The purple-podded bean* *tones well with the mauve heads of alliums, while the jagged grey leaves of the cardoon in front make a startling contrast. (p.154)*

WASH-DAY RUNNERS

Above. *Runner bean 'Painted Lady', an old cultivar with red and white flowers, looks more handsome than those with plain red flowers. Runner beans need plenty of root space, so this old zinc wash-* *tub is ideal and it cost me next to nothing. The courgette plant 'Gold Rush' at the bottom really needs a sunnier spot, though it has still managed to bear a couple of golden fruits. (p.155)*

AUTUMN HARVEST

Above. *The first ripe blackberries signify that summer's end is within sight, but at least the luscious fruit is a consolation. Cultivated blackberries can be trained against a sunny fence, and they produce much bigger and better fruits than the wild brambles. (p.155)*

GREEN SHADE

Above. *In many Mediterranean countries, the grape vine here is used to cast a gentle shade in which to sit on hot, sunny days. The thought of relaxing in one of these chairs, occasionally reaching up to pluck a few grapes, conjures up a vision of delicious idleness. (p.155)*

FRUITFUL TOWER POTS

Opposite. *Strawberries are one fruit that I couldn't be without in the garden. A stacking towerpot like this, from which the fruits dangle enticingly, will give you plenty of servings and the only space you need is a small sunny corner. (p.155)*

HANDY HERB BOX

Opposite. *Just open the kitchen window, reach out and pick a few leaves of whatever herb you need. Variegated lemon balm for a refreshing pick-me-up tea or a few leaves of chives to snip up and scatter over salads or new potatoes. This window-box has all these and lots, lots more. A few alpine strawberries tumble over one corner, while trailing plants – including golden creeping Jenny and nasturtiums – cascade over the front to conceal the box itself. (p.155)*

TAPESTRY OF THYME

Above. *Thymes love a sunny site and well-drained soil, so they are perfect for pots, and here several different kinds have been planted together to give a pretty, patchwork effect. Because thymes do not have deep roots, shallow containers such as this weathered terracotta pan are ideal. They are also excellent plants for the edges of containers. Warmed by the sun, the aromatic foliage will give off a lovely scent when crushed, and bees often visit the clusters of pink flowers. (p.155)*

CENTRE-STAGE TOMATOES

Opposite. *Rather than relegating tomatoes to some tucked-away corner and propping them up with old bamboo canes, try giving them a high-profile position on a stylish* support such as this handsome wrought-iron framework. After all, what could be more eye-catching than these bunches of tempting, ripe fruit? (p.155)

TOMATO AND PARSLEY BASKETS

Above. *Who said hanging baskets were just for flowers? Out of the five baskets which hang from this archway, it is the stunning pairing of vegetables and herbs that really draws the eye. This mouth-watering 'Tumbler' tomato is just one of a new generation of compact, trailing* vegetables that have been specially bred for containers. Crisp, furled parsley leaves are handy to have near the kitchen as well. This most useful of herbs can be put in various dishes or sauces; or sprigs of foliage can be used as a fresh garnish for all sorts of dishes. (p.155)

CLASSIC FAVOURITES
Roses

o flower epitomizes the midsummer garden so well as the rose. The full-petalled luxuriance of its blooms, often coupled with a delicious fragrance, is inseparable from that time of year when the days are long and the garden is at the peak of perfection. But comparatively few gardeners have the space – or indeed the desire – for the old-fashioned beds of roses that are so labour-intensive and look so stark in the winter. Fortunately, the newer roses of today and the many different climbing and rambling roses are ideal for integrating with other plants all round the garden.

For the hanging garden there are plenty of climbers and ramblers to choose from which scramble upwards and can be trained over all manner of supports. Like other climbing plants, these roses are incredibly versatile and can be used in many different places – against walls and fences, over pergolas, arches and arbours, into trees, and up posts and pillars. To create instant height in a border, there are weeping standards – rambler roses which the nurseryman has grafted onto a stem about 1.5 metres (5 feet) high – to create a luxuriant globe of colour. Lastly, there are ground-cover roses with a trailing and spreading habit.

Ground-cover roses are relative newcomers to the gardening scene. A number of spreading roses

SPECTACULAR PARTNERSHIP

Twined together in a spectacular embrace, clematis makes the perfect partner for a rose. It can also be used to extend the flowering season by choosing one, or more, that blooms before or after a rose. (p.155)

were introduced during the 1980s, though the majority of these were fairly vigorous and only suitable for larger banks and borders. However, recent years have seen the arrival of a new breed of compact, spreading, repeat-flowering roses that can be grown in hanging baskets, window-boxes and other containers. Chief among these are the County roses – named after the counties of England – which flower from mid- to late summer. Some of the most successful to date in hanging baskets have been 'Hertfordshire' with bright pink blooms and 'Suffolk' which has glowing scarlet flowers with a central mass of golden stamens. Also a good choice for baskets is 'Flower Carpet' with its large clusters of double or semi-double flowers in pure white or bright pink. In hanging baskets and other containers, roses are best grown on their own.

The difference in growth habit between climbing and rambler roses influences their choice for certain sites. Ramblers bear their flowers on long, flexible, quick-growing stems that have been produced in the previous year. The flowered stems are best pruned out at or near ground level each year in late summer. So ramblers are ideal for growing up posts, pergolas, arches, tripods, and other supports such as trees, where flexibility is a priority. Climbers, on the other hand, form a permanent framework of fairly rigid branches from which the flower-bearing sideshoots are produced. This type of rose is better on walls and fences where the stems can be trained and left undisturbed.

Depending on your preferences, you may want to opt for either the old-fashioned type of rose whose flowers are a sumptuous mass of petals crammed together, or modern climbers of comparatively recent introduction which have more open, sculpted blooms, similar to those of hybrid tea roses. The advantage of the modern climbers, which include favourites such as 'Compassion', 'Golden Showers' and 'Pink Perpétué', is that they have a fairly compact habit and produce repeated flushes of blooms throughout the summer, whereas many old-fashioned climbers and ramblers have one marvellous burst of colour lasting for several weeks.

Choosing the best roses for your garden is not a job to do in a hurry. Start with a good browse through a pile of catalogues which usually contain stacks of useful information and colourful pictures – this is an enjoyable job for long, dark winter evenings when you can lose yourself in visions of next summer's glory. Of course, no catalogue description can ever do a rose justice, and it is even better to spend time visiting gardens to see – and smell – roses 'in the flesh'.

Vigour and eventual size are important points to consider. Some ramblers in particular are incredibly vigorous and grow to an enormous size, flinging their branches over anything within reach with great exuberance. Chief among these rampant ramblers is 'Wedding Day', which bears masses of fragrant, creamy yellow flowers that turn white with age, and 'Bobbie James' with large white flowers. Also worth mentioning here is the most famous member of a small group of climbing rose species, *Rosa filipes* 'Kiftsgate'. This beautiful creamy white rose has an almost legendary vigour. It has been known to spread as much as 15 metres (50 feet). A large and well-established tree is essential to host one of these magnificent monsters.

A good feature to look for in a rose is some natural resistance to disease. This is one of my priorities as, like many people, I hate using chemicals in my garden. The attribute of disease-resistance can tip the balance away from some roses like 'Zéphirine Drouhin' and 'Dorothy Perkins' which, despite their lovely flowers, are martyrs to mildew.

The choice of plants to grow underneath and alongside a rose makes the difference between it looking simply attractive or absolutely stunning. At ground level first, there are plenty of perennials and small shrubs that can blend perfectly to create a 'cottage-garden' carpet of colour. Silver-foliaged plants like the woolly-leaved lamb's ears, *Stachys byzantina* (*S. lanata*), and the filigree foliage of *Artemisia*, contrast well with blue lavender, purple-leaved sage, *Salvia officinalis* 'Purpurascens' and even chives, *Allium schoenoprasum*. The onion smell of chives and the white liquid given off by their roots is said to help prevent black-spot disease.

Some low clumps of spiky foliage supplied by irises and *Sisyrinchium striatum* make a good contrast to rounded and mat-forming plants. Going upwards, tall spires of foxglove can mingle among the rose branches; and for an exquisite evening scent, sow some seed of the biennial sweet rocket, or dame's violet, *Hesperis matronalis*. The tendency of the latter to sprawl can be averted by tucking the stems discreetly amongst those of the rose, but I forgive this plant anything for the delicious perfume of its mauve or white flowers. Tall, graceful lilies are the ideal associates for summer, especially the richly fragrant regal lily, *Lilium regale*.

If space allows, there is no reason why a few rose branches can't be permitted to trail along the ground and thread their way through the border plants, so clusters of roses can pop up alongside the complementary perennials. Likewise, a ground-cover rose planted on top of a bank can be left untrained to tumble down the slope over a weed-suppressing bark mulch.

In many ways roses are perfect for a hanging garden: festooning pergolas, pillars and boundary walls, smothering impossible slopes and spilling from baskets. The choice is vast. Gardeners can opt for the best of the old, tried-and-tested varieties or sample some of the many exciting new introductions that continue to arrive on the scene. With roses abounding, there should never be any shortage of summer – and autumn – colour.

THE COUNTY 'SUFFOLK'

The newer ground-cover roses such as the County series are repeat-flowering with a compact habit which makes them ideal for hanging baskets and containers. This example is 'Suffolk'. (p.155)

VIGOROUS RAMBLER

Left. *The rose gardens at David Austin's nursery are a treasure trove of colour and fragrance. The stout, brick-pillared pergola needs to be strong to support 'Paul's Himalayan Musk', one of the giants of the rambler family. However, a similar effect can be created on a smaller scale using a less vigorous example. (p.156)*

COTTAGE GARDEN BEAUTY

Above. *This avenue of* Rosa 'Sanders' White Rambler', *underplanted with lavender, demonstrates how effective it is to use* en masse *a very limited choice of plants. These weeping standards formed by grafting rambler roses onto tall stems, bear little resemblance to the 'lollipops' often seen in formal gardens. (p.156)*

ROSE-CLAD RAILINGS

Opposite. *Iron railings can look rather bare, but spectacular climbing rose 'Chaplin's Pink Climber' has been allowed to grow over them to create a lovely, informal hanging garden. (p.156)*

SCENTED SEAT

Left. *Who could resist a seat beneath this delightfully fragrant canopy of* Rosa *'Félicité et Perpétué'? This old rose, introduced in 1827, is still one of the best ramblers for the garden. (p.156)*

MID-SUMMER GLORY

Below. *'Blairii Number 2' festoons rustic arches with flowers, mostly borne in one glorious mid-summer flush. Coppery young foliage and a delicious scent ensure this rose earns its place in the garden. (p.156)*

THE CHARM OF THE WILD
Wild flowers and natives

ot all that many years ago there was no shortage of plants growing in the wild. An abundance of copses, hedgerows, roadside verges and fields were full of flowers. In addition there were plenty of odd, derelict corners where plants were allowed to grow as they pleased. But the march of so-called progress has changed all that, as increasing amounts of land disappear under tarmac and concrete or have been turned over to 'productive' crops.

As a child, my playground was an old beech and oak woodland, carpeted with bluebells in spring and packed with birds. Now all that has gone, replaced by a dense, almost lifeless plantation of pines and larches. Sadly, it is only in nature reserves that most people can see the full beauty of wild flowers.

However, the tide of opinion is turning. More and more people are now growing native plants in their own gardens as well as supporting their conservation in the wild. It is now illegal in the most part to dig up plants from the countryside. In any case, it is best never to take plants from the wild. Doing so is inexcusable as there are plenty of nursery-raised plants available. Former ecologist Marney Hall, who is manager of Countryside Wild Flowers nursery and one of Britain's leading wild flower specialists, believes that when people can no longer look over their fences and see a mass of wild

WILD WALL POT

The delicate beauty of wild flowers is revealed at close quarters in a terracotta wall pot. Red poppies and valerian contrast well with the golden flowers of creeping Jenny and birds-foot trefoil. (p.156)

flowers, then they will grow them in their gardens. It was on this premise that she started the nursery six years ago. Once-common plants like cowslips, primroses, bluebells and violets, sell in far greater numbers in cities than in the country because, so Marney believes, people there are starved of native wild flowers. In fact, so much have opinions changed that gardeners are now asking for daisies to plant *in* lawns, whereas a few years ago they would have been spraying them with weedkiller.

Contrary to many people's beliefs, there is no need to have a big garden in order to grow wild flowers. They adapt to small-space and container gardening as well as any other plants, and in some cases, even better. In shady places, for example, you can grow woodland wild flowers like primroses, violets, red campion and bugle in troughs or baskets. There is herb Robert, or *Geranium robertianum*, with evergreen foliage that develops lovely red tints in autumn. Ground ivy, *Glechoma hederacea*, produces long trailing stems with scalloped leaves that have a pungent, minty smell when crushed. The variegated form has been a popular hanging basket plant for many years. There are also native ferns such as the hart's tongue fern and common polypody, which are covered in more detail on page 70.

Marney also stresses that there is no need to be purist with wild flower displays. Bedding plants can be included too, though it would be wise to choose them carefully. Formal plants with brightly coloured flowers, like busy lizzies, red pelargoniums and petunias, are obvious non-starters because of the harsh contrast they would make to the fragile charm of wild flowers. However, there are many which are suitable: pastel-coloured fuchsias, violas and pansies with plain 'faces', and single-flowered white miniature roses are a few examples. Pale blue lobelia and white alyssum would mix well with trailers.

Wild flowers are not just fair-weather plants either, for there are plenty that can be used in containers for winter and early spring interest. Here are just some of Marney's recommended plants for the colder months. For the tops of baskets or containers, there is her favourite heartsease, or wild pansy, (*Viola tricolor*), sweet violet (*V. odorata*) which often flowers from mid-winter through to spring, as do primroses (*Primula vulgaris*) in a sheltered spot. Though parsley is not a British native, it adds useful foliage interest and is a handy herb to have near the kitchen door. Small bulbs such as snowdrops or crocuses can be tucked in and around the plants at the top. For trailing evergreen foliage there is creeping thyme (*Thymus polytrichus*), common ivy (*Hedera helix* subsp. *helix*), or one of its many variegations, and wild strawberry (*Fragaria vesca*) whose leaves develop wonderful red tints in autumn. It has delicious summer fruits too, though you will have to be quick off the mark to pick them before the birds do!

It is not just people that appreciate wild flowers. Wildlife benefits too: from butterflies and bees feasting on nectar and pollen-rich flowers, to birds feeding on seeds and fruits. But sometimes birds even take up residence in a display, as Marney has found on several occasions. Originally her suspicions were aroused when she watered a hanging basket next to the kitchen window, because a wren would often fly out. It was not until winter came and all the foliage died back that she saw a beautifully constructed nest on the underside of the basket. Wrens also use their nests for winter roosts, so Marney left the basket in place and watched every evening as up to half a dozen birds squeezed into the tiny nest for warmth at night. With a well-stocked bird table nearby and a regular water supply, the local birds recognize a good patch when they see one. Even special dietary preferences are catered for: teasels are stuck in the ground around the bird table for seed-eaters such as goldfinches; the prickly seed-heads also deter cats.

Marney also becomes involved with diverse projects, from roadside plantings and large-scale landscaping to the showcase of the gardening world, the Chelsea Flower Show. Wild flower gardens to which she has contributed are a breath of country air at the annual show in the heart of London, and they have been awarded four gold medals and the most coveted prize of all, the Fiskar's Sword of Excellence for the best garden in the show.

The run-up to Chelsea is a test for the strongest nerves. Every plant needs to be at its peak of perfection, with some coaxed early into flower in heated greenhouses and others held back in cold storage. However, whereas many growers resort to high-tech solutions, Marney uses less orthodox methods which she discovered quite by accident whilst visiting her Buddhist acupuncturist: 'Spring was late a couple of years ago and hardly anything showed any colour two weeks before Chelsea. I was absolutely desperate. Then my acupuncturist asked whether I had actually told the plants what I wanted them to do? So at that point I thought anything was worth a try!

'That weekend I went into the greenhouse like Basil Fawlty, shouting "Right! Flower, or it's weed-killer for the lot of you!" And by Monday they had gone absolutely mad – I don't know whether it was the threat of death or the promise of glory. Now I tell my Chelsea plants they're going to be loved and admired by thousands of people, and they always do incredibly well.' Whatever the methods used to prepare the plants, I am immensely pleased that the Chelsea wild flower gardens have been so successful, introducing thousands of people to their unique charms. Whether you just want to enjoy their dainty beauty purely on its own merits, or use wild flowers as part of a wider plan to make your hanging garden more appealing to wildlife, there is something in these displays for everyone.

A Breath of Country Air

This glorious jumble of wild flowers could easily bring a breath of country air to a town garden. The trailers are left in place all year while the top planting is changed according to the season. (p.156)

SEASIDE MEMORIES

Opposite. *A glimpse of thrift conjures up visions of cliffs studded with cushions of pink flowers. This adaptable plant flourishes on rock walls and in baskets. Its flowers are popular with bees and butterflies. (p.156)*

EASY-GOING TOADFLAX

Above. *Ivy-leaved toadflax has been made more welcome in the garden than other members of its family which the plant hunter Reginald Farrer described as 'more toad than flax'. (p.156)*

OVERFLOWING FUMITORY

Clumps of yellow fumitory,
Corydalis lutea, *spill out of an old
bath, seemingly under direction
from the stone cherub. The name
'fumitory' derives from the word*
fumiterre *or 'earth smoke', due to
an old belief that corydalis arose
spontaneously without seed, and also
for its ancient use as a fumigant to
exorcize evil spirits. It is an easy-
going plant that self-seeds freely,
popping up almost anywhere in the
garden. It thrives in sun or shade
and colonizes cracks in walls and
paths, but I forgive it any invasive
tendencies because its cheerful
flowers are borne in profusion
through most of the year. (p.156)*

YEAR ROUND HEARTSEASE

Right. *The wild pansy or heartsease is one of Marney Hall's favourite flowers for containers as it blooms virtually all year round. It can even be relied on to supply a few flowers at Christmas. Here they have self-seeded into the gravel to colonize this small corner. (p.157)*

CLUSTER OF FACES

Above. *Seen at closer quarters, it is possible to pick out the detail on the tiny 'faces' of the heartsease and to see that each one is subtly different. In this little wall pot, heartsease is underplanted with a 'skirt' of creeping thyme whose shoots will soon grow down. (p.156)*

Part Three

PRACTICAL MATTERS

*I*n the preceding chapters, the illustrated plantings show a glorious and varied array of plants used in many exciting ways – from stunning single-species containers to carefully chosen combinations of plants that alternatively tone and contrast with each other. To help you put together the displays that have taken your fancy, the following pages provide all the background information that you will need: from container size and plant preferences for sun or shade, to diagrams of the more complex plantings so you can see exactly which plants are which.

Here too is the nitty-gritty practical information on how to plant and care for your displays in order to get the very best results. Containers are covered in detail and because they offer limited growing space, the plants are dependant on you for the essentials of life. More than in any other type of gardening, the secret of successful container displays – and especially hanging baskets – is the quality and frequency of the care that they receive. Finally, there is a list of suppliers for the containers and plants featured in this book.

There are no great secrets, no 'muck and magic', to successful gardening. My advice is just to follow the basic guidelines for planting and maintenance, recreate the planting suggestions here or use them as a basis for your own ideas, but most of all, enjoy yourself!

A BLOOMING WATERFALL

So many flowers are packed under the window of the Woodman Inn, Hampshire, that they appear to tumble out of the window-box in a glorious waterfall of colour; held in check only by an apron of busy lizzies. (p.157)

THE CHOICE OF CONTAINERS

Starting with hanging baskets, these can be divided into two types: solid and open-mesh. Solid ones are essentially suspended plant pots which do not need to be lined. Open-mesh baskets are much more versatile as the sides and base can be planted as well as the top, but a liner is needed to retain compost and plants. The vast majority of hanging baskets are made of plastic or plastic-covered wire, and these are the most inexpensive. Their appearance is of little importance as a well-planted basket should soon be hidden under a mass of foliage. Where the basket has a higher profile, you could consider a handsome one made of wrought iron. Woven wire baskets are exceptionally elegant and stylish, though if you are investing in a handmade container of this sort, the planting needs to be minimal and carefully chosen in order to show off the workmanship.

Hanging baskets are usually suspended from brackets fixed to walls, posts or pergolas, though it is also possible to have a free-standing display by using a hanging-basket 'tree'. There are designs available that can take anything from two to ten baskets. On a similar note, there are jardinières – essentially a basket on a stand – which make superb moveable displays of trailing plants.

There are lots of different containers that can be fixed to walls or fences. Wall pots come in a range of styles from plain plastic to beautifully designed terracotta. Swags are tough growing bags in a variety of shapes, from half-moon garlands to long tubes used to swathe a drainpipe. They are versatile and a cheap way of growing plants in all sorts of places.

Tall pots, urns, chimney pots and olive oil jars are all ideal for trailing plants and terracotta pots come in a variety of designs. Tall pots are not only perfect for the patio as a background to smaller containers, but they can also be stood in a border to provide some instant height.

I love using all sorts of old, throw-away things as cheap and cheerful containers. Vegetable racks can be fixed to a wall and filled with trailing plants. Old zinc dolly tubs are ideal for deep-rooted climbers like runner beans and courgettes. Sinks, toilets, old boots and watering cans can all be pressed into service; they are sure to raise a smile too.

HANGING BASKET LINERS

Although sphagnum moss has traditionally been used for lining baskets, it is harvested from fast-dwindling bogs and other wild areas, so I prefer to use an alternative, preferably one which is made from recycled material. Wool-based liners are very good at retaining water, and they also supply some nitrogen to the plants. Coir (coconut-fibre) liners are available as solid, fibrous, brown mats, and as a dyed-green 'moss' which looks quite unobtrusive and is reusable. There are also liners which are made from foam and cardboard. Pre-formed liners come in different sizes, so make sure you select the right one for your basket. It is best to choose a material that looks fairly natural, although the plants should conceal the liner in a relatively short space of time.

PLANTING A WIRE-MESH BASKET

An hour or so before you begin, give all the plants a really good soaking in a bucket of water so their rootballs are saturated. The soaking not only helps the plants withstand the shock of transplanting, but also dry rootballs are very hard to re-wet once planted. First, sit your basket on a bucket or a large pot for stability while you work and position the lining material. If you are using moss, press a generous layer over the basket and put a circle of polythene in the bottom to help retain water. Then fill about a third of the basket with compost.

The secret of successful hanging baskets is to cram them with as many plants as possible so, starting at the base, make holes at regular intervals in the liner and insert a trailing plant through each hole. Young plants with small rootballs are best for planting through the sides and base, and it also helps to squeeze and compact the rootball in your hand first. It can then be slipped in with little danger of damage. Continue to plant through the sides, adding compost in stages as you work up the basket. The plants used for the top of the basket can be larger and more established than those for the sides, as the size of their rootball is no problem. For a balanced appearance, put the tallest plants in the centre. Firm the compost gently with your fingers, but take care not to over-compact soil-less composts.

The basket can be hung in its final position so long as there is no danger of frost damage to tender plants (see page 139). Hang it up before watering as the compost will soak up lots of water and the basket will become much heavier to lift. Alternatively, water before hanging up, allowing any excess to drain, to ensure the compost is wet through. Use a watering can with a fine rose to give the basket a thorough and gentle watering to settle the compost around the plant roots. Top up the compost if it sinks and leaves any large gaps.

Be warned about buying tender plants too soon as garden centres tend to have frost-tender annuals and perennials on sale very early in the season. By all means buy them early if you have a greenhouse or conservatory where plants can be protected. Baskets and containers can be planted up and the display starts to establish itself for several weeks before going outside. It is important to acclimatize the plants to the outside world gradually over a week or two by putting them out during the day and bringing them back in at night. However if a display of tender plants has to go outside immediately after planting, patience is the watchword. Do not be tempted to put such a display out in mid-spring, even if the weather is warm and sunny, as there may well be a late frost that will severely check or even kill tender plants. It is far better to let the nurseries take the risk and delay planting containers until late spring when all danger of frost is past.

PLANTING CONTAINERS

Containers that have been used previously are best scrubbed out using hot, clean water and a stiff brush, as any residual debris can harbour pests and diseases. Stone and terracotta containers are porous, so before planting, soak them in water for an hour or so first or they will 'steal' water from the compost. To reduce water loss through the growing season, line the sides (but not the base) of large containers with a thick (about 1 cm/ ½ in) layer of newspaper. Small containers and wall pots are better lined with plastic film or sheeting.

Check that pots, window-boxes and any other containers you intend to plant have drainage holes. If none are present some will have to be made to allow excess water to drain away. If the roots are sitting in water for any length of time, they will be deprived of air and this will eventually cause them to rot and the plant to die. To ensure free drainage, put a layer of broken crocks or pieces of polystyrene in the base of the container. Pots standing on a solid surface also need some provision to prevent the compost becoming waterlogged, so raise the containers just a centimetre or so (about 1 in) off the ground so surplus water can flow away. You can buy ornamental pot feet, but some flat stones or old tiles placed underneath the pot will do the job just as well.

Raised beds need to have 'weep holes' at the base to allow excess water to drain out. It is also wise to put a 10 cm (4 in) layer of crocks or rubble in the bottom. Cover this with coarse leafmould or plastic mesh to prevent the compost washing down and clogging the drainage holes.

Whatever the type of container, never be tempted to skimp on the compost or the results of your work could be disappointing. Bear in mind that in a confined space,

plants need to get their roots into something good in order to perform well for months or even years.

I prefer to use peat-free composts like those made from recycled materials such as coir. Being relatively light, these soil-less composts are best for baskets and other hanging containers where weight is an important consideration. Weight isn't a problem with pots that stand on the ground, and here I prefer to use the loam-based John Innes composts, as the loam they contain provides more of a buffer against drought than soil-less composts. There are few lime-hating trailing plants, but those such as gentians and *Lithodora (Lithospermum)* will need a special lime-free, or ericaceous, compost.

There are two exceptions to using one-hundred-per-cent fresh potting compost in containers. One is with very large pots, where a half-and-half mix of potting compost and well-rotted garden compost will give good results. The other is with bulbs, as they effectively contain all the nutrients they need, and so they can be planted in the compost from old growing-bags or that used for summer-flowering plants. However, the old compost should be mixed with an equal amount of fresh.

WATERING

The importance of regular watering cannot be over-emphasized, especially for hanging baskets, wall pots and other suspended containers. They dry out very rapidly because the whole rootball is exposed to sun and quick-drying breezes. In addition, containers positioned against house walls receive very little rain.

Because all container-grown plants have a limited root space, the compost dries out quickly. Never rely on rain alone to provide for your plants as the canopy of foliage usually prevents most of it from reaching the compost. On that note, do not forget to check the need for watering even during wet weather.

It is difficult to give an exact guide to watering because weather, location, aspect and other factors of each individual site affect the amount of water your plants will need. However, as a general guide, hanging containers and small pots will need watering at least once, and more probably twice, a day during hot, sunny weather. If by any mischance a hanging basket dries out completely, take it down and give it a good soaking in a bucket of water for an hour or two. If possible, water your plants in the evening as less water will be lost through evaporation.

Although I enjoy the daily routine of watering, it is a time-consuming job and, if I am away for even a day, I need to arrange for someone else to do it. So I have installed an automatic watering system. There are some excellent and reasonably priced systems now available that have been specially designed for the ordinary garden. Automatic watering saves time, which can then be spent doing something else, or just sitting and relaxing.

It is possible to buy a tap-mounted water-timer in order to pre-programme the watering times, so your system becomes fully automatic – ideal for holidays. Such a system can look complex at first glance, but setting it up is quite straightforward. Basically you need a 'mains' pipe to run from your tap around the area to be watered, and from this pipe run small 'spaghetti' lines which are pegged onto each container. These lines terminate in little drip heads that deliver a about a litre (2 pints) of water per hour. This gentle delivery is much better for the plants than an occasional gush from a hose.

Before buying and setting up an irrigation system, position your containers exactly where you want them, measure up roughly how much hose you will need and check the number of containers to be watered. It is best to install your system on a warm, sunny day so the pipes are flexible. First set out the mains pipe so it is as unobtrusive as possible, usually along the base of a wall. Where there are a number of hanging baskets on the same wall, run the pipe in a straight line above the baskets, which probably means between ground- and first-floor windows. Use right-angled joints to fit the pipe snugly around corners. Then fix the spaghetti lines, concealing them as much as possible. If the joints and drip heads are hard to put in, dip the pipe ends in a pan of near-boiling water to make them more flexible.

Frequency of watering will vary depending on the site and weather conditions. It is best to experiment to see how long it takes to give your containers a good soaking. Working on the little-and-often principle, I set the timer to water in the early morning and in the evening, sometimes with a midday top-up if the weather is really hot and breezy.

FEEDING

All container-grown plants need regular feeding during the growing season – from spring to autumn. There are two options: regular applications of liquid fertilizer or a controlled-release fertilizer added to the compost at planting time. Liquid fertilizers need to be diluted with water and applied once or twice a week. Flowering plants need a fertilizer high in potash, such as a tomato fertilizer, to boost the production of flowers and fruits.

With summer-flowering annuals, it is a good idea to switch to a high-nitrogen fertilizer in late summer to encourage a final burst of growth.

Controlled-release fertilizer has been used widely by professional growers for years but only recently has it become available to gardeners. It comes in the form of pellets or small granules coated in a slow-dissolving resin which is temperature-sensitive, so nutrients are only released when the plants are actively growing. Although it works out a bit more expensive, I prefer to use this method as it saves the weekly job of liquid feeding. The nutrients last for most of the season, though they can become exhausted towards the end of summer, and then it is worth applying a few liquid feeds.

CARE OF PERMANENT DISPLAYS

Permanent plants – such as shrubs, herbaceous perennials and ornamental grasses – in containers benefit from a little attention each spring to keep them at their best. If possible, gently scrape off the top few centimetres (about 2 in) of compost and replace it with fresh. The same feeding options apply as outlined above: either mix some controlled-release fertilizer in with the top-dressing of new compost, or apply a weekly liquid feed. However, it is best not to feed permanent plants after mid- to late summer, as the nutrient boost will encourage the growth of soft shoots that could be damaged by frost.

Plants will not perform at their best once they have become pot-bound and their container packed with roots. Once this stage is reached, either move the plants out to the border or pot them up into a larger container. Perennials and grasses can be rejuvenated by dividing their rootstocks into several pieces, discarding the old, woody centre and replanting the smaller divisions.

WINTER CARE AND PROTECTION

Containers that remain outdoors all year need to be tough enough to withstand winter frosts. Not all terracotta is frost-proof, an important point to consider when buying pots.

Good drainage is especially important during the winter months, as the water in over-wet compost will freeze and probably damage both the roots and the container. Bear this in mind at the planting stage and ensure the pots have a generous layer of drainage material. They should also be raised off the ground (see page 139).

In very cold weather the roots of all container-grown plants will be vulnerable to frost damage because the whole rootball is above ground. It is well worth insulating the pots as a temporary measure when hard frosts are forecast. First, move the pots close together, which will give a degree or two rise in temperature, and if possible move them against the house wall for added protection. Wrap the pots with insulating material such as bubble plastic or hessian sacks stuffed with straw. It is also worth protecting the foliage of evergreens by wrapping it in bubble plastic or horticultural fleece; the leaves can become scorched by bitterly cold winds. Remember to take off the covering as soon as the weather improves. Snow is a wonderful natural insulator, so let it lie on the plants unless its weight is in danger of damaging them.

Do not overlook the need for a little watering during the winter months, especially for containers in sheltered sites. But only water them sparingly if the compost is drying out or the weather is very cold.

Depending on your locality, frost-tender plants may need to be moved into a greenhouse, porch or conservatory. In colder areas only the hardiest plants can remain outside through the winter; tender ones will need to be kept under cover in a frost-free environment. However, it is possible to overwinter tender plants in an unheated structure, though do bear in mind that survival cannot be guaranteed. Insulate the structure with bubble plastic and, most importantly, keep the compost very much on the dry side as too much moisture is a killer.

Fortunately most frost-tender perennials can be easily raised from cuttings. Take cuttings of non-flowering shoots in late summer. These will root during winter if kept in a conservatory or on a well-lit windowsill.

CLIMBING PLANTS

Advance ground preparation pays dividends with all garden plants, and especially so with climbers that will be growing against walls or fences. The soil in such places tends to be on the dry side because the wall or fence shields the ground from rain. With new houses in particular, the soil near walls is often poorer than elsewhere in the garden. So before planting, dig a hole about two spades deep and at least 60 cm (2 ft) across and dig in a couple of buckets of organic matter. Well-rotted manure, garden compost or spent mushroom compost are ideal, as are the many packaged planting composts. Add some slow-release fertilizer, unless you are using a packaged compost which already contains some feed.

Soak the rootball, complete with pot, in a bucket of water for an hour or so before planting. Then knock out the plant and unwind some of the roots if they have formed a tight coil at the base. Put the plant in the hole

so its roots are at least 30 cm (1 ft) away from the base of a wall or fence, and lean it towards its support. Always put a plant in the ground so it remains at the same depth as it was growing previously. The exception is large-flowered hybrid clematis which are best planted about 10 cm (4 in) deeper than before. Then, if the plant is attacked by clematis wilt – a fairly common and non-preventable disease – it will nearly always regrow from below the ground. Finally, backfill the hole, firming the soil around the plant with your heel, and water well. Keep the plant well watered during any dry spells. Autumn is by far the best time of year to plant, because the soil is warm and moist, which is ideal for root growth. During mild spells during the winter, the roots will continue to grow and so the plant will be well established in time for an explosion of growth in the spring. However, there is no problem in planting container-grown plants at any time of year, so long as they are thoroughly watered in dry weather.

SUPPORTS FOR CLIMBERS

With the exception of self-clinging climbers like ivies *(Hedera)* and *Parthenocissus*, all plants will need some sort of framework on which to climb. Wires run between vine eyes (screws with a loop at the end) are cheapest and least obtrusive. On walls, sink the vine eyes into the brick, rather than the mortar, and run the wires close to the mortar courses. Space the wires about 30 cm (1 ft) apart, and always use good quality galvanized wire as it will probably be there for many years.

Trellis is the other popular option with a whole range of styles and prices to choose from. To fix trellis to a fence or wall, first screw on wooden battens about 2.5 cm (1 in) thick. Mount the trellis panels on the battens which will allow space for the plants to twine.

Climbers need not be limited to walls and fences. They can grace pergolas, arches. arbours, tripods and obelisks. With all these structures, it is important that they are sturdy enough to carry the weight of the plants. Vigorous climbers such as *Clematis montana* will soon form a dense mass of foliage which is not only heavy, but will also be buffeted by strong winds. Other climbers like wisterias will develop substantial stems in time.

Wooden supports for large structures are best sunk at least 45 cm (18 in) into the ground. Dip the end in wood preservative, rather than just paint them, to delay rotting as long as possible. A longer lasting alternative is to set posts in concrete or to use long metal spikes with a hole in the top to take the post.

Key to the Plantings

CONTAINERS
Type 2 wire hanging baskets
Size 30cm (14in)

PLANTING
Deciduous climbers grown by Will Tooby and Angie Fuller of Bransford Garden Plants. To create the 'ball', two wire hanging baskets are each planted with a clematis and left to grow on for several weeks so the roots can establish. The two baskets are then wired together to form a sphere, with the plant stems emerging from the join. Subsequently, the growth is wound around the basket to create a mass of flowers and foliage.
Position part or full shade
Plants 2 *Clematis* 'Silver Moon'

GROUP PLANTING
A collection of summer containers, planted in spring by Val Charrington at Horsebridge Station, Kings Sonborne, Hampshire.
Position sunny or part shade

CONTAINER A
Type 3 wire hanging baskets
Size 35cm (14in)

CONTAINER B
Type 12 assorted individual pots placed on an old handcart
Size 1.5m (5ft)

CONTAINER C
Type 2 chimney pots
Size height 60cm (2ft), width 23cm (9in)

Page 2

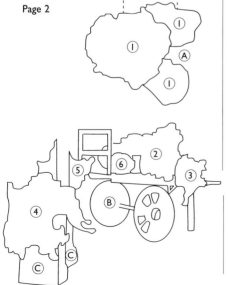

Key to plants
1. 60 *Impatiens* Accent Series
2. 9 *Pelargonium* mixed cvs.
3. 3 *Pelargonium* 'Rosais'
4. 1 *Petunia* 'Surfinia Purple'
5. 1 *Fuchsia* cv.
6. 1 *Tolmiea menziesii*

CONTAINER
Type 3 plastic pots in a woven wire plant holder, hand-made by Celestino Valenti
Size 8–13cm (3–5in)

PLANTING
A summer display of flowers and foliage planted in spring.
Position sunny
Plants
Above 1 *Pelargonium* 'Bruni'
Below 2 *Hedera helix* subsp. *helix* 'Gold Ingot'

GROUP PLANTING
Massed display of summer bedding plants in various containers planted in spring and grown at the Woodman Inn, Durley, Hampshire, by landlord Tony Senger.
Position sunny

CONTAINER A
Type 3 wooden half-barrels
Size height 38cm (15in), width 60cm (2ft)

CONTAINER B
Type 50 plastic pots massed on the ground, some of which are sitting on other, upturned pots
Size 10cm (4in)

Key to plants
1. 3 *Calceolaria integrifolia* 'Sunshine'
2. 3 *Argyranthemum* 'Royal Yellow'
3. 50 *Impatiens* 'Rose Star' and 'Super Elfin Swirl'
4. 5 *Petunia* 'Express White'
5. 4 *Pelargonium* 'Cramden Red'
6. 15 *Impatiens* Accent Series
7. 1 *Pelargonium* 'Rouletta'

CONTAINER C
Type window-box made from old scaffolding boards
Size length 1m (3ft 3in), width and height 20cm (8in)

Key to plants
8. 1 *Calceolaria integrifolia* 'Sunshine'
9. 3 *Lobelia* 'Lilac Fountain'
10. 3 *Begonia* 'Non-stop Red'
11. 3 *Begonia* 'Non-stop Pink'
12. 3 *Begonia* 'Non-stop Yellow'

13. 1 *Helichrysum petiolare* 'Variegatum'
14. 2 *Fuchsia* cvs. (trained in bush form)
15. 3 *Pelargonium* 'Rouletta'

CONTAINER D
Type old cast-iron hay rack
Size width 45cm (18in)

Key to plants
16. 3 *Calceolaria integrifolia* 'Sunshine'
17. 7 *Lobelia* Fountain Series
18. 8 *Impatiens* Accent Series
19. 1 *Helichrysum petiolare*
20. 3 *Fuchsia* 'Swingtime'

CONTAINER E
Type 5 wire hanging baskets
Size 40cm (16in)

Key to plants
21. 3 *Pelargonium* 'Mrs Parker' and 2 *Pelargonium* 'Cherry Sundae'
22. 5 *Pelargonium* 'Tiberias'
23. 5 *Fuchsia* mixed trailing cvs.
24. 9 *Lobelia* Fountain Series
25. 5 *Pelargonium* 'Leucht Cascade'
26. 1 *Scaevola aemula* 'Blue Fan'
27. 3 *Pelargonium* 'Sassy'
28. 3 *Fuchsia* trailing cv.
29. 3 *Pelargonium* 'Lilac Cascade'
30. 3 *Petunia* mixed hybrids
31. 5 *Pelargonium* 'Tiberias'
32. 5 *Pelargonium* 'Leucht Cascade'

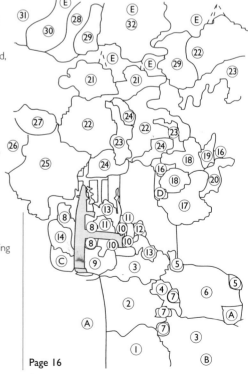

Page 16

BASKETS AND BOXES
Annuals and bedding plants

These seasonal displays in hanging baskets and window boxes are mostly planted out in late spring for summer colour. In colder areas containers can be planted in early spring and kept under cover if space allows. Hang them outside when all danger of frost is past.

Page 18	Photographed mid-August

CONTAINERS
Type 2 troughs
Size 75cm long, 20cm high and 23cm wide (30 × 8 × 9in)

PLANTING
A summer display of bedding plants in two troughs, planted in spring and growing at the Sun Inn, Dorset.
Position sunny

Key to plants
1. 1 *Pelargonium* 'Belvedere Glory'
2. 3 *Lobelia* 'White Fountain'
3. 1 *Viola* 'Ultima Yellow'
4. 13 *Petunia* mixed hybrids
5. 5 *Lobelia* Fountain Series
6. 3 *Lobelia* 'Rose Fountain'
7. 3 *Mimulus* 'Malibu Orange'
8. 1 *Fuchsia* bush cv.
9. 3 *Mimulus* 'Malibu Ivory'
10. 3 *Lobelia* 'Purple Fountain'

Page 18

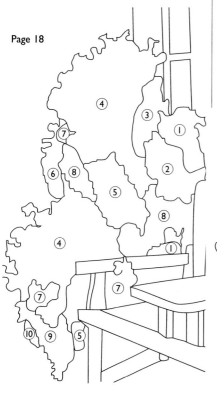

Page 20	Photographed early August

CONTAINER
Type wire hanging basket
Size 30 cm (12in)

PLANTING
A simple summer basket, planted in spring and grown by Colegrave Seeds.
Position part or full shade
Plants
Above 3 *Impatiens* 'Accent Pink'
Below 5 *Lobelia richardii*

Page 21	Photographed early August

CONTAINER
Type wire hanging basket
Size 35cm (14in)

PLANTING
A summer basket, planted in spring and grown by Colegrave Seeds.
Position sunny or part shade
Plants 3 *Impatiens* 'Rhapsody'

Page 22	Photographed early August

CONTAINER
Type wire hanging basket
Size 35cm (14in)

PLANTING
A summer basket, planted in spring and grown by Colegrave Seeds.
Position sunny
Plants 5 *Pelargonium* 'Ville de Dresden'

Page 23	Photographed mid-July

CONTAINER
Type wire hanging basket
Size 35cm (14in)

PLANTING
A basket for summer display hanging from a wooden pergola. Planted in spring and grown by Jane Lees at the Brickmaker's Arms, Windlesham, Surrey.
Position sunny

Page 23

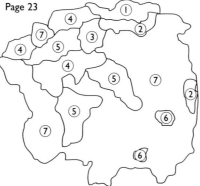

Key to plants
1. 3 *Pelargonium* 'Purpurba'
2. 3 *Pelargonium* 'Rosais'
3. 3 *Impatiens* 'Double Pink'
4. 7 *Impatiens* 'Picotee Swirl'
5. 7 *Lobelia* 'Sapphire'
6. 5 *Impatiens* 'Tempo Rose'
7. 7 *Lobelia* 'Lilac Wonder'

Pages 24–5	Photographed mid-July

CONTAINERS
Type 3 wire hanging baskets
Size 35cm (14in)

PLANTING
A row of three summer baskets, grown by Jane Lees (as Page 23).
Position sunny or partial shade

Key to plants
1. 21 *Lobelia* 'Sapphire'
2. 6 *Helichrysum petiolare* 'Variegatum'
3. 5 *Petunia* Double Madness Series (rose and white)
4. 15 *Impatiens* 'Deco Pink'
5. 5 *Pelargonium* 'Palais'
6. 5 *Pelargonium* ivy-leaved cv.
7. 5 *Pelargonium* 'Lachkönigen'
8. 3 *Fuchsia* 'Princessita'
9. 7 *Petunia* Double Madness Series (silver shades)

Pages 24–5

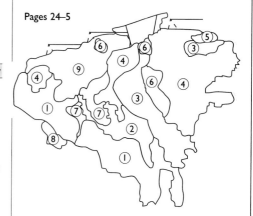

Page 25	Photographed late May

CONTAINER
Type wire hanging basket
Size 35cm (14in)

PLANTING
An early-summer basket, planted in early spring and grown under cover until danger of frost had passed.
Position sunny or partial shade

Key to plants
1. 1 *Solenopsis axillaris*
2. 1 *Bidens aurea*

3. 7 *Viola* 'Universal Purple'
4. 7 *Viola* 'Universal Yellow'
5. 3 *Fuchsia* pale pink cvs.
6. 7 *Viola* yellow cv.
7. 5 *Lobelia* 'Sapphire'
8. 3 *Helichrysum petiolare*
9. 3 *Verbena* 'White Knight'

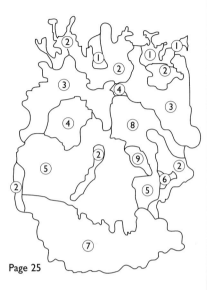

Page 25

Page 26	*Photographed early August*

CONTAINERS
Type 2 wire hanging baskets
Size 35cm (14in)

PLANTING
Two summer baskets planted in spring and suspended on Hi-lo devices for easy winching up or down.
Position sunny

Key to plants
1. 6 *Helichrysum petiolare*
2. 3 *Thunbergia alata*
3. 5 *Petunia* purple and white hybrids
4. 6 *Pelargonium* 'Belvedere Glory'
5. 5 *Pelargonium* ivy-leaved cv. (pink)
6. 7 *Lobelia* 'White Fountain'
7. 7 *Lobelia* 'Crimson Fountain'
8. 5 *Petunia* red hybrids
9. 1 *Verbena* 'Silver Anne'

Page 26

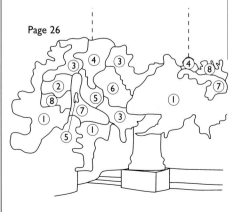

Page 27	*Photographed early August*

CONTAINER
Type wire hanging basket
Size 35cm (14in)

PLANTING
A summer basket of trailing begonias, raised from seed and planted in spring by Colegrave Seeds.
Position sunny or part shade
Plants 5 *Begonia* 'Illumination Pink'

Page 28	*Photographed mid-November*

CONTAINER
Type wire hanging basket
Size 30cm (12in)

PLANTING
An autumn/winter basket lined with conifer clippings, planted in summer and grown by John Glover.
Position sunny or shade

Key to plants
1. 3 *Brassica oleracea* purple form
2. 3 *Erica gracilis* var. *alba*
3. 3 *Erica gracilis*
4. 3 *Hedera helix* subsp. *helix* 'Chicago Variegated'
5. 2 *Hedera helix* subsp. *helix* 'Kolibri'

Page 28

Page 29	*Photographed early August*

CONTAINERS
Type wire hanging basket
Size 30cm (12in)

PLANTING
A summer basket with foliage providing the dominant theme, planted in spring and grown by Brian Smith of Woodlea Nurseries.
Position partial shade

Key to plants
1. 3 *Plecostachys serphyllifolia*
2. 3 *Helichrysum petiolare*
3. 5 *Brachyscome multifida*
4. 3 *Felicia amelloides* variegated
5. 1 *Plectranthus forsteri* 'Marginatus'
6. 7 *Impatiens* 'Accent White'
7. 3 *Lobelia* 'Riviera Blue'

Page 29

Pages 30–1	*Photographed late May*

CONTAINER
Type window-box
Size length 75cm (30in), height and depth 20cm (8in)

PLANTING

A summer display, planted in early spring and grown under cover until all danger of frost had passed.
Position sunny

Key to plants

1. 2 *Thuja orientalis* 'Aurea Nana'
2. 3 *Pelargonium* 'Dark Red Irene'
3. 3 *Pelargonium* 'Charlotte Bronte'
4. 3 *Pelargonium* 'A Happy Thought'
5. 5 *Impatiens* red cv.
6. 2 *Pelargonium* 'Golden Staph'
7. 3 *Tradescantia zebrina*
8. 3 *Fuchsia* trailing cvs.
9. 3 *Lobelia* Fountain Series
10. 3 *Lysimachia nummularia* 'Aurea'
11. 3 *Hedera helix* subsp. helix 'Gold Ingot'
12. 2 *Lamium maculatum*

Page 31	*Photographed late May*

CONTAINER

Type window-box
Size length 75cm (30in), height and depth 20cm (8in)

PLANTING

A summer display, planted in early spring and grown under cover until danger of frost had passed.
Position sunny

Key to plants

1. 9 *Argyranthemum foeniculaceum*
2. 3 *Petunia* lemon hybrid
3. 5 *Impatiens* 'Accent White'
4. 3 *Helichrysum petiolare* 'Limelight'
5. 5 *Glechoma hederacea* 'Variegata'

ANYTHING GOES

Annuals and bedders in unusual containers

These displays are either planted in spring for summer colour, or in early autumn for autumn and winter colour. The young shrubs and conifers used in some of the displays can be re-used for several seasons until they become too large. Then they can either be planted out in the garden or moved on to a larger container.

Page 32	*Photographed early August*

GROUP PLANTING

Novel containers filled with summer bedding, planted in spring and grown by Brian Smith of Woodlea Nurseries. The 'swag bag' of busy Lizzies is described below, in the entry for Page 42 (see page 147).
Position part or full shade

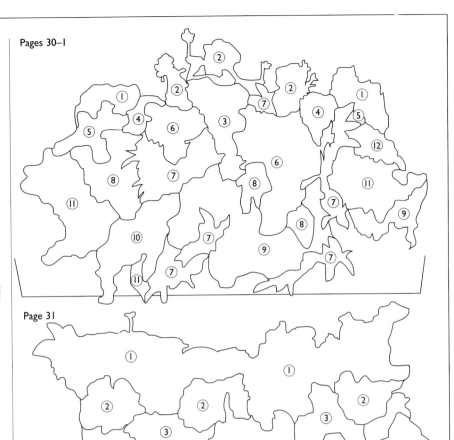

Pages 30–1

Page 31

Page 32

CONTAINER A

Type old toilet basin
Size height 40cm (16in), width 25cm (10in)

CONTAINER B

Type hand-painted bucket
Size height and width 28cm (11in)

Key to plants

1. 1 *Chamaecyparis lawsoniana* 'Lane'
2. 3 *Impatiens* 'Accent Bright Eye'
3. 1 *Impatiens* 'Ambience'
4. 3 *Hedera helix* subsp. helix 'Goldchild'
5. 6 *Lysimachia nummularia* 'Aurea'
6. 3 *Lobelia* 'Lilac Fountain'
7. 3 *Lonicera nitida* 'Baggesen's Gold'
8. 1 *Impatiens* 'Ambrosia'
9. 1 *Begonia* 'Finale'
10. 1 *Thymus* x *citriodorus* 'Silver Queen'

GROUP PLANTING

A display of summer flowers and foliage, planted in spring and grown by Brian Smith of Woodlea Nurseries.
Position sunny or part shade

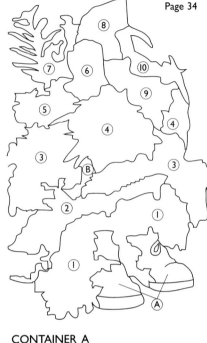

Page 34

CONTAINER A
Type old pair of boots
Size height 15cm (6in), width 15cm (6in)

CONTAINER B
Type galvanised bucket
Size height 25cm (10in), width 30cm (12in)

Key to plants
1. 2 *Ajuga reptans* 'Multicolor'
2. 2 *Sedum lineare* 'Variegatum'
3. 3 *Hedera helix* subsp. *helix* 'Adam'
4. 1 *Impatiens* 'Ambrosia'
5. 1 *Tagetes* 'Safari Yellow'
6. 1 *Pelargonium* 'Dolce Vita'
7. 1 *Lonicera nitida* 'Baggesen's Gold'
8. 1 *Chamaecyparis lawsoniana* 'PemburyBlue'
9. 1 *Solenostemon (Coleus)* green-and-white-foliage selection
10. 1 *Solenostemon (Coleus)* purple-foliage selection

GROUP PLANTING

Assorted containers filled with bedding plants and conifers for autumn display, planted in summer and grown by Brian Smith. The conifers are tall-growing cultivars and will only be suitable for small containers for a year or two, when they will need to be potted on, planted out in the border, or discarded.

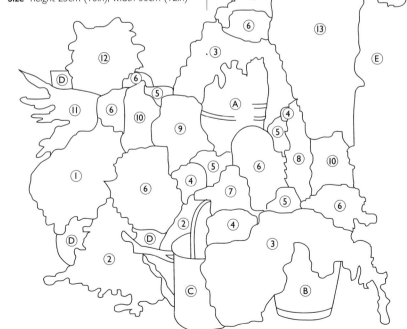

Page 35

Position sunny or partial shade

CONTAINER A
Type old milk churn
Size height 1m (3ft), width 18cm (7in)

CONTAINER B
Type hand-painted bucket
Size height 38cm (16in), width 28cm (11in)

CONTAINER C
Type hand-painted watering-can
Size height 28cm (11in), width 23cm (9in)

CONTAINER D
Type 3 terracotta pots
Size height 28–32cm (11–13in), width 28–38cm (11–15in)

CONTAINER E
Type brickbuilt raised bed
Size height 132cm (52in), width 79cm (31in)

Key to plants
1. *Chamaecyparis obtusa* 'Pygmaea'
2. 2 *Hedera helix* subsp. *helix* 'Adam'
3. 5 *Hedera helix* subsp. *helix* 'Goldchild' and 'Buttercup'
4. 4 *Viola* 'Ultima Sherbet'
5. 5 *Viola* 'Ultima Chiffon'
6. 10 ornamental kale 'Northern Lights'
7. 1 *Chamaecyparis pisifera* 'Boulevard'
8. 3 *Chamaecyparis lawsoniana* 'Columnaris'
9. 1 *Chamaecyparis lawsoniana* 'Allumii'
10. 2 *Chamaecyparis lawsoniana* 'Stewartii'
11. 2 *Lonicera nitida* 'Baggesen's Gold'
12. 1 *Chamaecyparis lawsoniana* 'Lane'
13. 1 *Hedera helix* subsp. *helix* 'Chicago Variegated'

CONTAINERS
Type 400 plastic pots
Size 10cm (4in)

PLANTING

A colourful mixture of summer plants raised from seed, all grown in individual pots around Fey Hasan's first-floor balcony.
Position sunny

Key to plants
1. 90 *Tropaeolum majus* mixed
2. 130 *Impatiens* mixed
3. 50 *Lobelia* Fountain Series
4. 25 *Cleome hassleriana* 'Colour Fountains'
5. 20 *Tagetes* mixed French marigolds
6. 30 *Pelargonium* mixed cvs.
7. 30 *Dahlia* mixed seed raised
8. 15 *Petunia* mixed cvs.
9. 10 *Celosia argentea* var. *cristata* Plumosa group

CONTAINER
Type wooden boat
Size height 1m, (3ft 3in), length 2.4m (8ft)

PLANTING
A summer display of flowering annuals, seed-raised in spring.
Position sunny
Plants 30 *Tropaeolum majus* mixed cvs.

CONTAINER
Type plastic pot wedged in neck of urn
Size 23cm (9in)

PLANTING
Flower and foliage plants for early summer colour, planted in spring.
Position part shade

Plants
Above   1 *Pelargonium* 'Frank Headley'
Centre   3 *Lewisia cotyledon* hybrids
Below   1 *Hedera helix* subsp. *helix* 'Chicago Variegated'

GROUP PLANTING
Bedding plants for summer display, planted in spring and grown by Lynda Brown.
Position sunny

CONTAINER A
Type plastic pot in neck of stone urn
Size 18cm (7in)

CONTAINER B
Type terracotta pot
Size height 20cm (8in), width 15cm (5in)

Key to plants
1. 3 *Lobelia* 'Riviera Sky Blue'
2. 1 *Pelargonium* 'Lachskönigin'

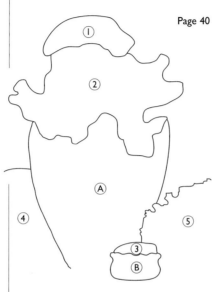

Page 40

3. 1 *Mentha requienii*
4. *Bergenia cordifolia* 'Purpurea' (in border)
5. *Geranium* × *oxonianum* 'A.T. Johnson' (in border)

GROUP PLANTING
Mixed bedding plants, tender perennials and shrubs for summer flowers, planted in spring and grown by Lynda Brown.
Position sunny

CONTAINER A
Type plastic pot wedged in neck of old Greek olive-oil jar
Size 23cm (10in)

CONTAINER B
Type 3 terracotta pots
Size height 20cm (8in), width 25cm (10in)

Page 41

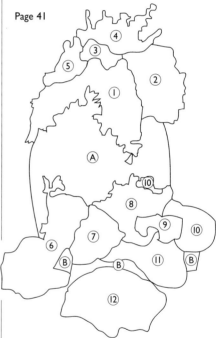

Key to plants
1. 3 *Fuchsia* 'Gay Fandango'
2. 1 *Pelargonium* 'Harvard'
3. 1 *Lobelia* 'Riviera Sky Blue'
4. 1 *Helichrysum petiolare* 'Limelight'
5. 1 *Pelargonium* 'White Queen'
6. 3 *Petunia* mixed hybrids
7. 1 *Pelargonium* 'Mrs Cannel'
8. 1 *Fuchsia* 'Genii'
9. 1 *Lobelia* 'Riviera Sky Blue'
10. 1 *Pelargonium* 'Lachskönigin'
11. 1 *Osteospermum* 'Weetwood'
12. *Dianthus* 'Doris' (in border)

Pages 36–7

Page 42 — *Photographed late July*

CONTAINER
Type hanging 'swag bag'
Size height 45cm (18in), width 30cm (12in)

PLANTING
A hanging bag filled with trailing lobelia for summer colour, planted in spring. The bag is filled evenly with compost and laid flat on the ground. Make three or four punctures in the underside for drainage. On the top side and using a sharp knife, make T-shaped cuts at 8–10cm (3–4in) centres, so the T will be upside down when the bag is hanging up. Young plants (often called plugs) are best to use as their rootballs are small. Plant the bag, working from the outside to the centre. When complete, water the bag thoroughly and leave it lying flat for several weeks, so the plants can establish a good root system before the bag is hung up.
Position part shade
Plants
Top 15 *Lobelia* 'Blue Fountain'
Centre 10 *Lobelia* 'White Fountain'
Bottom 5 *Lobelia* 'Purple Fountain'

Page 43 — *Photographed mid-August*

CONTAINER
Type wall basket
Size height 20cm (8in), width 38cm (15in)

PLANTING
A summer display of shrubs and perennials planted in spring.
Position part shade
Plants
Top 1 *Sambucus racemosa* 'Tenuifolia'
Centre 3 *Fuchsia* 'Cascade'
Bottom 5 *Lysimachia nummularia* 'Aurea'

Page 44 — *Photographed mid-August*

CONTAINER
Type flower pouch
Size length 1m (3ft 3in)

PLANTING
A summer display of busy Lizzies, planted in spring. For planting instructions see Page 42 (above).
Position part or full shade
Plants 36 *Impatiens* in mixed colours

Page 45 above — *Photographed mid-August*

CONTAINER
Type swag 'Drop 45'
Size height 45cm (18in)

PLANTING
A summer display of busy Lizzies, planted in spring and grown by Brian Smith. For planting instructions see Page 42 (above).
Position part or full shade
Plants 25 *Impatiens* 'Accent Bright Eye'

Page 45 below — *Photographed mid-August*

CONTAINER
Type 'swag' bag
Size width 1m (3ft 3in)

PLANTING
A summer display of busy Lizzies, planted in spring and grown by Brian Smith. For planting instructions see Page 42 (above).
Position part or full shade
Plants
Outside 35 *Impatiens* 'Accent Red'
Centre 8 *Impatiens* 'Accent White'

WHAT GOES UP . . .
Climbers and trailers

All permanent plants growing in a border will benefit from an application of slow-release fertilizer and a top dressing of well-rotted manure or compost in spring. The latter is especially important for climbers as the soil at the bases of walls and fences tends to be drier and poorer than elsewhere in the garden.

Page 46 — *Photographed early June*

PLANTING
Deciduous and hardy climber planted permanently in a border and trained against a wall. Buy grafted plants, as seed-raised wisterias can take many years to flower. For best results, prune twice a year. In midsummer, shorten long sideshoots to five or six buds from the main stem. In the middle of the following winter, these same shoots can be shortened again, to two or three buds.
Position full sun
Plant 1 *Wisteria sinensis*

Page 48 — *Photographed mid-June*

PLANTING
Deciduous herbaceous climber growing permanently in the border. It dies back in winter, when all the stems can be cut back to the ground.
Position sunny or light shade
Plant 1 *Humulus lupulus* 'Aureus'

Page 49 — *Photographed early August*

PLANTING
Deciduous, perennial climber that dies down over winter, planted permanently in a border and trained over a clipped yew hedge.
Position part shade in moisture-retentive soil
Plants 3 *Tropaeolum speciosum*

Pages 50–1 — *Photographed early October*

PLANTING
Hardy evergreen and deciduous climbers planted in a border against a wall.
Position part or full shade
Plants
Top left 1 *Hedera helix* subsp. *helix* 'Goldheart' (adult form)
Below left 1 *Hedera hibernica*
Centre 1 *Parthenocissus quinquefolia* (red foliage)
Right 1 *Hydrangea anomala* subsp. *petiolaris* (yellow foliage)

Page 51 — *Photographed mid-June*

PLANTING
Hardy deciduous self-clinging climber growing permanently in a border by a wall.
Position part or full shade
Plant 1 *Hydrangea anomala* subsp. *petiolaris*

Page 52 — *Photographed mid-August*

CONTAINER
Type wire hanging basket
Size 35cm (14in)

PLANTING
Hardy, deciduous climbers, one in a basket, the other planted permanently in a border by a wall at Bransford Garden Plants.
Position sunny or shade
Plants
1 *Campsis* x *tagliabuana* 'Madame Galen'
1 *Parthenocissus tricuspidata* 'Veitchii' (in basket)

Page 53 — *Photographed late September*

PLANTING
Hardy, deciduous self-clinging climber planted permanently in a border by a wall.
Position sunny or shade
Plant 1 *Parthenocissus quinquefolia*

Page 54 — *Photographed late August*

PLANTING
An annual climber raised from seed under cover in early spring and planted out into the border in late spring.
Position sunny
Plants 3 *Ipomoea quamoclit* (*Mina lobata*)

Page 55 — *Photographed mid-August*

CONTAINER
Type wooden basket of 'burst seed pod' design
Size height 25cm (10in), width 45cm (18in)

PLANTING
Hardy deciduous climber and herbaceous perennial in a hanging basket by Will Tooby and Angie Fuller of Bransford Garden Plants. Given an annual top dressing of fertilizer and compost (see page 140), the plants should

grow well in this container for several years.
Position sunny or shade
Plants
Above | *Hosta fortunei* var. *aureomarginata*
Below | *Vitis coignetiae*

Page 56   *Photographed mid-September*

PLANTING

Hardy deciduous climber growing in a border.
Prune back to 45cm (18in) above the ground
in late winter.
Position sunny or part shade
Plant | *Clematis* 'Kermesina'

Page 57   *Photographed late May*

PLANTING

Annual climbers raised from seed under
cover and brought on early for the Chelsea
Flower Show. Normally sweet peas are plant-
ed out in spring for a summer display.
Position sunny
Plants 20 *Lathyrus odoratus* mixed colours

Page 58   *Photographed mid-August*

PLANTING

Hardy deciduous climber and summer bed-
ding growing in a border in the garden of
Kerry and Linda Pitter.
Position sunny
Plants
Above | *Clematis* 'Bees' Jubilee'
Below 9 *Impatiens* Rosette Series

Page 59   *Photographed mid-August*

PLANTING

Deciduous hardy climbers forming 'balls' as
described for Page 1 planting (see page 142).
Plants
Left 2 *Clematis* 'Sunset'
Right 2 *Clematis* 'Silver Moon'

Page 60   *Photographed late May*

PLANTING

Hardy deciduous climber growing against a
wall. Prune immediately after flowering only if
necessary to contain rampant growth.
Position sunny or shade
Plant | *Clematis montana* 'Tetrarose'

Page 61   *Photographed mid-May*

PLANTING

Hardy deciduous climber growing permanently in the border by a doorway. If plant
becomes overgrown or too vigorous, prune
hard immediately after flowering.
Position sunny or shade
Plant | *Clematis montana*

Page 62   *Photographed mid-August*

CONTAINER
Type cast-iron urn
Size height 1m (3ft 3in), width 45cm (18in)

PLANTING

Hardy deciduous climbers planted for spring
and summer display at Bransford Garden
Plants. Hard prune *Clematis montana* immediately after flowering. The hybrid clematis is
pruned in late winter. Top-dress annually with
fertilizer and compost as described on page
140 to keep this display growing well for a
number of years.
Position part shade
Plants | *Clematis* 'Comtesse de Bouchaud'
(in summer flower)
| *Clematis montana* var. *rubens* (spring
flowers over)

Page 63   *Photographed early September*

CONTAINER
Type stoneware urn
Size height 38cm (15in), width 23cm (9in)

PLANTING

Hardy deciduous climber for summer display
at Bransford Garden Plants. Prune hard in
late winter and topdress as described on
page 140.
Position part or full shade
Plant | *Clematis* 'Elsa Späth'

Pages 64–5   *Photographed late September*

PLANTING

A vigorous, hardy, deciduous climber and
half-hardy evergreen climber planted permanently in a border and loosely trained over a
fence. If necessary, prune back both plants in
early spring.
Position sunny
Plants
| *Clematis tangutica* (yellow flowers)
| *Eccremocarpus scaber* (orange flowers)

Page 66   *Photographed early July*

PLANTING

Herbaceous perennial climber planted permanently in the border at Burford House
Gardens, Worcestershire. The plant dies back
during winter, when the dead stems can be
cut back to the ground.
Position sunny
Plant | *Lathyrus rotundifolius*

Page 67   *Photographed late May*

PLANTING

Hardy deciduous foliage climber growing in a
border and trained over a wrought-iron
framework made by Agriframes. The yellow
flowers belong to a laburnum.
Position sunny
Plant | *Actinidia kolomikta*

ELEGANT FOLIAGE, COOL CONTRASTS
Ferns and grasses

All the plants featured here are hardy
and perennial. With a little care, they
can be kept in containers indefinitely.
For two or three years after planting, a
spring top-dressing of compost and
fertilizer (see page 140) will keep
them in good condition. Once a plant
has outgrown its container, either pot
it on into a larger one, or, in spring,
divide it into several smaller clumps
and replant them.

Page 68   *Photographed mid-August*

GROUP PLANTING

A selection of hardy ornamental grasses and
foliage plants at Bransford Garden Plants.
Position part or full shade

CONTAINER A
Type terracotta imitation chimney pot
Size height 45cm (18in), width 15cm (6in)

CONTAINER B
Type wooden hanging basket
Size height 25cm (10in), width 45cm (18in)

Key to plants
1. | *Carex elata* 'Aurea' (*C. stricta* 'Bowles'
Golden')
2. | *Hosta fortunei* var. *aureomarginata*
3. | *Vitis coignetiae*
4. | *Carex riparia* 'Variegata'

Page 68

Page 71 — *Photographed mid-August*

GROUP PLANTING
Hardy ornamental grasses growing at Bransford Garden Plants.
Position sunny or part shade

CONTAINER (left)
Type stoneware urn
Size height 60cm (24in), width 25cm (10in)
Plant 1 *Leymus arenarius*

CONTAINER (right)
Type terracotta imitation chimney pot
Size height 45cm (18in), width 15cm (6in)
Plant 1 *Carex elata* 'Aurea' (*C. stricta* 'Bowles' Golden')

Page 72–3 — *Photographed mid-August*

CONTAINER
Type imitation wrought-iron wall trough from the Erin Blacksmith range
Size height 18cm (7in), width 55cm (22in)

PLANTING
Hardy evergreen fern and trailing herbaceous perennial.
Position shade
Plants
Above 1 *Asplenium scolopendrium*
Below 3 *Lamium galeobdolen* 'Florentinum' (*L. galeobdolen* 'Variegatum')

Page 74 — *Photographed late-August*

CONTAINER
Type imitation wrought-iron wall basket
Size height 20cm (8in), width 38cm (15in)

PLANTING
Hardy ornamental grass underplanted with yellow-leaved trailing hardy perennial.
Position part shade
Plants
Above 1 *Hakonechloa macra* 'Aureola'
Below 3 *Lysimachia nummularia* 'Aurea'

Page 75 — *Photographed mid-August*

GROUP PLANTING
A mixture of hardy perennials and ornamental grasses.
Position shade

CONTAINER A
Type imitation wrought-iron wall trough
Size height 18cm (7in), length 55cm (22in)

CONTAINER B
Type terracotta long-tom
Size height 32cm (13in), width 28cm (11in)

Page 75

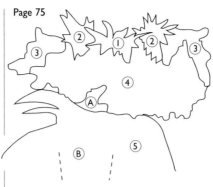

Key to plants.
1. *Hosta* 'June'
2. 2 *Ophiopogon planiscapus* 'Nigrescens'
3. 2 *Viola riviniana* Purpurea Group (*V. labradorica purpurea*)
4. 3 *Ajuga reptans* 'Multicolor'
5. 1 *Hakonechloa macra* 'Aureola'

Pages 76–7 — *Photographed mid-August*

CONTAINER
Type stone 'head of David' fixed to wall
Size height and width 23cm (9in)

PLANTING
Hardy ornamental grass for permanent display, grown by John Glover.
Position part shade
Plant 1 *Carex conica* 'Snowline'

HEARTY HALF-HARDIES
Fost-tender perennials

These summer-flowering plants can be treated as bedding plants in colder areas, and planted out in late spring. However, they can also be kept over winter in a frost-free greenhouse or conservatory. If these facilities are not available, most tender perennials can be propagated easily from cuttings taken in autumn or early spring. In mild frost-free areas, the plants will survive outdoors all year.

Page 78 — *Photographed late-July*

CONTAINER
Type four-tier wire vegetable rack
Size each tray: length 1m (3ft 3in), height 13cm (5in), width 23cm (9in)

PLANTING
Tender perennials and annuals for summer display, planted in spring. Grown by Della Connolly.
Position sunny

Key to plants
1. 1 *Mimulus aurantiacus* var. *puniceus*
2. 1 *Pelargonium* 'Rosais'
3. 1 *Argyranthemum* cv. (pale yellow)
4. 3 *Lobelia* 'White Fountain'
5. 1 *Nemesia* 'Innocence'
6. 3 *Brachyscome multifida*
7. 3 *Petunia* pale pink hybrids
8. 3 *Convolvulus tricolor* (*C. minor*)
9. 1 *Bidens aurea*
10. 6 *Convolvulus sabatius*
11. 1 *Maurandya barclayana*
12. 1 *Rhodochiton atrosanguineus*
13. 1 *Nemesia* (seed raised)
14. 3 *Alonsoa warscewiczii* 'Peachy-Keen'
15. 3 *Persicaria elata* 'Pink Bubbles'
16 1 *Verbena* 'White Knight'
17. 5 *Lobelia* Fountain Series
18. 1 *Verbena* 'Silver Anne'
19. 1 *Brachyscome* 'Lemon Mist'
20. 1 *Diascia* 'Ruby Field'
21. 1 *Plectranthus forsteri* 'Marginatus'
22. 1 *Linum* cv.
23. 3 *Lysimachia nummularia* 'Aurea'

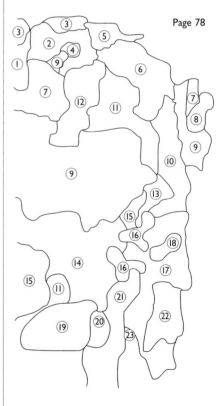

Page 78

Page 80 — *Photographed early August*

CONTAINER
Type wire hanging basket
Size 35cm (14in)

PLANTING
A summer basket of tender perennials planted in late spring, grown by Proculture Plants.
Position sunny or shade

Page 80

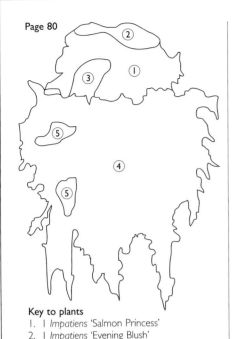

Key to plants
1. 1 Impatiens 'Salmon Princess'
2. 1 Impatiens 'Evening Blush'
3. 1 Impatiens 'Peach Ice'
4. 3 Plectranthus forsteri 'Marginatus'
5. 3 Sutera cordata 'Snowflake'

Page 82	Photographed late July

CONTAINERS
Type 2 wire trays, the smaller tray sitting directly on top of the larger tray
Sizes 120 × 75 × 15cm (48 × 30 × 6in); 120 × 45 × 15cm (48 × 18 × 6in)

PLANTING
Massed tender perennials planted in later spring for summer display, grown by Della Connolly.
Position sunny

Page 82

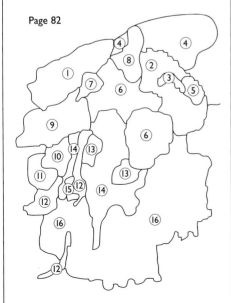

Key to plants
1. 3 Argyranthemum 'Vancouver'
2. 3 Argyranthemum 'Jamaica Primrose'
3. 1 Pelargonium red cv.
4. 1 Alonsoa warscewiczii 'Peachy-Keen'
5. 3 Brachyscome multifida
6. 1 Alonsoa warscewiczii
7. 1 Solenopsis (Isotoma) axillaris
8. 1 Fuchsia cv.
9. 5 Verbena 'Dema Purple'
10. 1 Nemesia caerulea
11. 1 Petunia striped hybrid
12. 1 Maurandya barclayana
13. 3 Brachyscome 'Lemon Mist'
14. 3 Plectranthus forsteri 'Marginatus'
15. 1 Mimulus aurantiacus var. puniceus buff form
16. 3 Petunia 'Surfinia Purple'

Page 83	Photographed early August

CONTAINER
Type wrought-iron jardinière
Size height 1m (3ft 3in), width 45cm (18in)

PLANTING
A summer foliage display of hardy and tender perennials, planted in late spring and grown by Proculture Plants.
Position part shade

Page 83

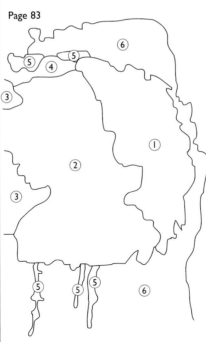

Key to plants
1. 5 Tolmiea menziesii
2. 5 Plectranthus forsteri 'Marginatus'
3. 5 Lamium maculatum 'Aureum'
4. 2 Helichrysum petiolare 'Limelight'
5. 3 Helichrysum petiolare
6. 3 Petunia 'Surfinia Purple' (in separate pot)
7. 5 Glechoma hederacea 'Variegata'

Page 84	Photographed late July

CONTAINER
Type wrought-iron jardinière
Size height 1m (3ft 3in), width 45cm (18in)

PLANTING
Freestanding container of tender perennial for summer display. and planted in late spring.
Position sunny

Key to plants
1. 3 Diascia barberae
2. 3 Verbena 'Sissinghurst'
3. 1 Helichrysum petiolare 'Limelight'
4. 3 Verbena purple cv.

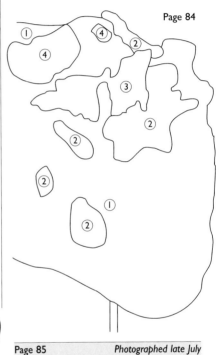

Page 84

Page 85	Photographed late July

GROUP PLANTING
A grouping of tender perennials in individual pots, planted by Rupert Golby and photographed at Whichford Pottery.
Position sunny

CONTAINER A
Type round terracotta flowerpot
Size height 15cm (6in), width 16cm (6½in)

CONTAINER B
Type terracotta rose bowl
Size height 21cm (8½in), width 30cm (12in)

CONTAINER C
Type terracotta flowerpot
Size height 38cm (15in), width 30cm (12in)

CONTAINER D
Type Italianate terracotta pot
Size 38cm (15in), width 53cm (21in)

CONTAINER E
Type terracotta 'orange' pot
Size height 56cm (22in), width 75cm (30in)

Key to plants
1. 1 *Thymus vulgaris albus*
2. 1 *Thymus vulgaris*
3. 1 *Thymus × citriodorus*
4. 1 *Verbena* 'Silver Anne'
5. 1 *Diascia* 'Ruby Field'
6. 1 *Bidens aurea*
7. 1 *Helichrysum petiolare*
8. 1 *Verbena* sp.
9. 1 *Argyranthemum* 'Blizzard'

Page 85

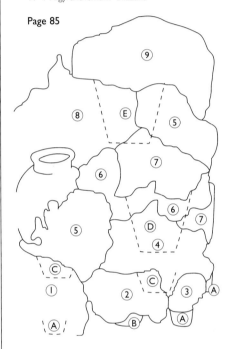

| Page 86 | *Photographed late July* |

CONTAINER
Type terracotta wall pot
Size height 24cm (9½in), width 28cm (11in)

PLANTING
Tender perennials planted in spring for summer display, grown by Rupert Golby and photographed at Whichford Pottery.
Position part shade
Plants
1 *Plecostachys serpyllifolia* (silver foliage)
1 *Verbena* 'Aphrodite' (pink flowers)

| Page 87 | *Photographed late July* |

CONTAINER
Type terracotta wall pot
Size height 24cm (9½in), width 28cm (11in)

PLANTING
A summer display of tender perennials planted in spring, grown by Rupert Golby and photographed at Whichford Pottery.
Position sun

Key to plants
1. 1 *Pelargonium* 'Breakaway Salmon'
2. 1 *Felicia amelloides* variegated
3. 1 *Viola* purple hybrid
4. 1 *Helichrysum petiolare* 'Limelight'
5. 1 *Bidens aurea*

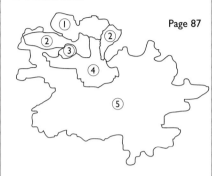

Page 87

| Page 88 | *Photographed late July* |

CONTAINER
Type chimney pot
Size height 75cm (30in), width 15cm (6in).

PLANTING
Tender perennial for summer display planted in spring by Della Connolly.
Position sun
Plant 1 *Diascia* 'Ruby Field'

| Page 89 | *Photographed late August* |

GROUP PLANTING
A grouping of Whichford pots filled with tender perennials, planted in spring and grown at Peter Higgs' nursery. The central pot at the rear is sitting on another, upturned for extra height.
Position sunny

CONTAINER A
Type terracotta long-tom
Size height 33cm (13in), width 23cm (9in)

Page 89

CONTAINER B
Type 2 terracotta lily pots
Size height 38cm (15in), width 30cm (12in)

CONTAINER C
Type small terracotta Ali Baba pot
Size height 27cm (11in), width 28cm (11½in)

Key to plants
1. 1 *Nemesia* 'Innocence'
2. 1 *Gazania* 'Dorothy'
3. 3 *Brachyscome* 'Lemon Mist'
4. 1 *Helichrysum petiolare*
5. 1 *Verbena* 'Silver Anne'
6. 1 *Verbena × maonettii*
7. 1 *Verbena* 'Pink Parfait'
8. 3 *Sutera cordata* 'Snowflake'
9. 3 *Brachyscome* 'Pink Mist'
10. 3 *Convolvulus sabatius*
11. 1 *Pelargonium* 'Galilee'
12. 1 *Fuchsia* pink-flowered cv.

| Page 90 | *Photographed early August* |

CONTAINERS
Type 2 wire hanging baskets
Size 35cm (14in)

PLANTING
Two baskets of tender perennials for summer display, planted in spring and grown by Proculture Plants.
Position sunny

Key to plants
1. 5 *Scaevola aemula* 'Blue Fan'
2. 3 *Lotus berthelotii*

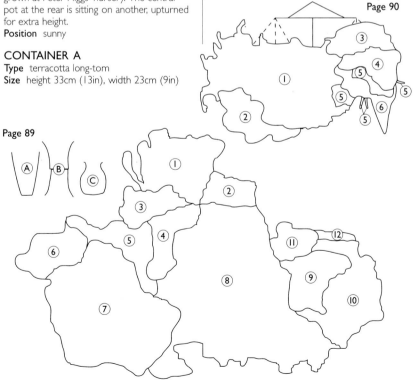

3. 3 *Impatiens* 'Cardinal Red'
4. 3 *Tropaeolum majus* 'Red Wonder'
5. 3 *Acalypha reptans* (*A. pendula*)
6. 3 *Abutilon megapotamicum* 'Variegatum'
Plus 3 *Lantana camara* and 3 *Begonia fuchsioides* (to flower later)

| Page 91 | *Photographed early August* |

CONTAINER
Type plastic pot
Size height 1m (3ft 3in), width 38cm (15in).

PLANTING
Tender perennials planted in spring for summer display, grown by Colegrave Seeds.
Position sunny
Plants 3 *Petunia* 'Surfinia Purple Mini'

| Page 92 | *Photographed late July* |

CONTAINER
Type stone urn
Size height 75cm (30in), spread 45cm (18in)

PLANTING
Tender perennials planted in spring for summer display, grown by Della Connolly.
Position sunny

Key to plants
1. 1 *Ricinus communis*
2. 1 *Streptocarpus saxorum*
3. 1 *Helichrysum petiolare*
4. 1 *Glechoma hederacea* 'Variegata'
5. 1 *Tropaeolum majus* 'Hermine Grashoff'
6. 1 *Petunia* 'Surfinia Pink Vein'
7. 1 *Alonsoa warscewiczii*
8. 1 *Nemesia caerulea*
9. 1 *Linum* sp.

Page 92

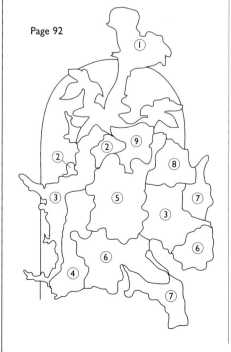

| Page 93 | *Photographed late May* |

CONTAINER
Type wire hanging basket
Size 30cm (12in)

PLANTING
An early summer basket of tender and hardy foliage plants planted under cover in early spring.
Position part shade

Key to plants
1. 3 *Chlorophytum comosum* 'Variegatum'
2. 5 *Hypoestes phyllostachya*
3. 3 *Hypoestes phyllostachya* 'Purpuriana'
4. 3 *Tolmiea menziesii*
5. 3 *Saxifraga stolonifera*
6. 3 *Hedera helix* subsp. *helix* 'Kolibri'
7. 1 *Ficus benjamina* 'Variegata'

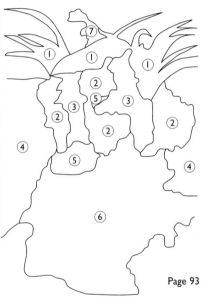

Page 93

SMALL-SCALE VERSATILITY
Perennials, alpines and shrubs

These hardy, perennial plants need little maintenance. In spring, plants growing in the border benefit from a top-dressing of fertilizer, while those growing in containers are best top-dressed with some fresh compost and fertilizer (see page 140). After flowering, trim off the dead flower heads, and cut dead herbaceous perennial foliage to the ground during winter.

| Page 94 | *Photographed late May* |

PLANTING
Alpines growing permanently in a rock bank.
Position sunny

Key to plants
1. 3 *Helianthemum* 'Henfield Brilliant'
2. 3 *Aurinia saxatilis* (*Alyssum saxatile*)
3. 3 *Helianthemum* 'Wisley Primrose'
4. 1 *Armeria maritima*
5. 2 *Phlox douglasii*
6. 3 *Oxalis tetraphylla*
7. 1 *Phlox subulata* purple form
8. 1 *Phlox subulata* pink form

Page 94

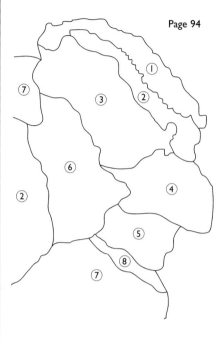

| Page 97 | *Photographed early September* |

CONTAINER
Type terracotta wall pot
Size height 15cm (6in), width 20cm (8in)

PLANTING
A succulent-leaved alpine for all-year-round display.
Position sunny
Plant 1 *Sempervivum tectorum*

| Page 98 | *Photographed mid-May* |

PLANTING
Detail of a rock garden with alpines.
Position sunny
Plant 1 *Aurinia saxatilis* (*Alyssum saxatile*)

| Page 99 | *Photographed mid-June* |

PLANTING
Detail of a rock garden with hardy perennial fern and alpine.
Position part shade
Plants
Left 1 *Gypsophila repens* 'Rosea'
Right 1 *Dryopteris filix-mas*

Page 100   *Photographed late June*

PLANTING
Hardy perennials allowed to self-seed in crevices around a flight of steps.
Position part shade
Plants
Above *Erigeron karvinskianus*
Below *Alchemilla mollis*

Page 101   *Photographed late September*

PLANTING
Ground-covering shrub in the border. In spring, prune the dead stems back to where fresh shoots are appearing.
Position sunny
Plant 1 *Ceratostigma plumbaginoides*

Page 102   *Photographed early May*

PLANTING
Perennial rock plant growing in a raised bed.
Position sunny or part shade
Plant 1 *Iberis sempervirens*

Page 103   *Photographed early June*

PLANTING
Hardy perennials growing in a dry-stone wall.
Position part shade
Plants
Above 1 *Geranium renardii*
Centre 1 *Campanula* sp.
Below left 1 *Corydalis ochroleuca (Pseudo-fumaria alba)*

Pages 104–5   *Photographed early November*

CONTAINER
Type window-box supported on brackets
Size length 120cm (4ft), height and width 20cm (8in)

PLANTING
Permanent planting of herbaceous perennials and shrubs for autumn and winter display, grown by John Glover. All but the heathers are completely frost-hardy.
Position sunny or part shade

Key to plants
1. 2 *Heuchera* 'Rachel'
2. 6 *Hedera helix* subsp. *helix* mixed cultivars

Page 104–5
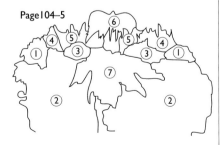

3. 2 *Gaultheria procumbens*
4. 2 *Erica gracilis* var. *alba*
5. 4 *Erica gracilis*
6. 1 *Carex conica* 'Snowline'
7. 1 *Juniperus horizontalis* Glauca Group

Page 105   *Photographed late May*

CONTAINER
Type window-box
Size length 75cm (30in), height and depth 20cm (8in)

PLANTING
Mixed perennials and annuals for an early summer display. Frost-tender perennials prolong the flowering period.
Position sunny or part shade

Key to plants
1. 3 *Argyranthemum* 'Chelsea Girl'
2. 2 *Felicia amelloides* variegated
3. 2 *Hosta* cv.
4. 2 *Miscanthus sinensis* 'Gracillimus'
5. 1 *Viola* 'Universal Yellow'
6. 1 *Viola* 'Universal Purple'
7. 1 *Helichrysum petiolare* 'Variegatum'
8. 3 *Hedera helix* subsp. *helix* (variegated)
9. 3 *Bidens aurea*

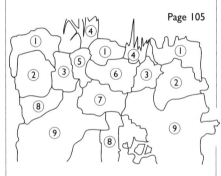

Page 105

A COOK'S DELIGHT
Vegetables, fruits and herbs

Vegetables can easily be raised from seed; either sow indoors in small pots during early spring, or directly in the growing position in early to late spring, according to the advice given on the packet. The hardy and perennials herbs and fruit plants listed below all benefit from fertilizing and top-dressing in spring. Top-dress those in the border with garden compost or manure, and those in containers with fresh potting compost.

Page 106   *Photographed late May*

CONTAINER
Type wire hanging basket
Size 30cm (12in)

PLANTING
A summer basket of annual salad vegetables, planted in late spring.
Position sunny
Plants
Top 1 tomato 'Tumbler'
Centre 7 lettuce 'Lollo Bionda'
Below 7 lettuce 'Lollo Rossa'

Page 109   *Photographed late May*

CONTAINER
Type terracotta pot by Althea Wynne
Size height 23cm (9in), width 60cm (24in)

PLANTING
Part of a garden of edible plants at the 1994 Chelsea Flower Show. Annual plants raised under cover and planted out in early spring.
Position sunny
Plants
Above 1 courgette
Below 7 *Tropaeolum majus* mixed cvs.

Page 110   *Photographed late May*

PLANTING
An ornamental mixture of decorative and edible plants growing in the border.
Position sunny

Key to plants
1. 1 tayberry
2. 2 purple-podded French beans
3. 1 *Cynara cardunculus* (cardoon)
4. 1 *Lunaria annuum*
5. 2 *Allium aflatunense*
6. 1 *Allium schoenoprasum* (chives)

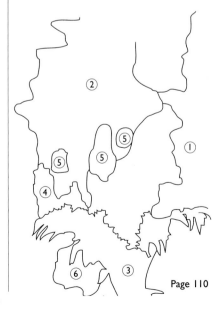

Page 110

Photographed mid-August

CONTAINER
Type zinc washtub
Size height 48cm (19in), width 40cm (16in)

PLANTING
Annual vegetables raised under cover and, planted out into a container in early summer.
Position sunny
Plants 5 runner bean 'Painted Lady'
Below left 1 courgette 'Gold Rush'

Page 112 *Photographed late May*

CONTAINER
Type plastic tower pot
Size height 1.2m (4ft), width 23cm (9in)

PLANTING
Perennial fruiting plant, raised under cover and planted out in spring for an early crop.
Position sunny
Plants 18 strawberry 'Royal Sovereign'

Page 113 left *Photographed mid-September*

PLANTING
Perennial cane fruits planted permanently in the border and trained against a fence. These are vigorous plants with a spread of 2.4–3m (8–10ft). Prune after harvest by cutting out the entire branch that has borne fruit. Pruning is easier if the new season's growth is kept separate from the fruiting branches.
Position sunny
Plant 1 blackberry 'Loch Ness'

Page 113 right *Photographed early August*

PLANTING
A perennial fruiting climber growing outside in a border and trained over the roof of a conservatory.
Position sunny
Plant 1 *Vitis vinifera*

Page 114 *Photographed late May*

CONTAINER
Type window-box
Size length 75cm (30in), height and depth 20cm (8in)

PLANTING
A summer display of annuals and perennials including many plants and herbs, planted in spring.
Position sunny

Key to plants
1. 1 alpine strawberry 'Baron Solemacher'
2. 1 *Pelargonium* 'Lady Plymouth'
3. 1 *Glechoma hederacea* 'Variegata'
4. 1 *Melissa officinalis* 'Aurea' (golden lemon balm)
5. 1 *Salvia officinalis* 'Icterina' (golden sage)
6. 1 *Lavandula stoechas*

7. 1 *Chamaemelum nobile* (chamomile)
8. 1 *Anthriscus cerefolium* (chervil)
9. 1 *Allium tuberosum* (garlic chives)
10. 1 *Foeniculum vulgare* (fennel)
11. 1 *Origanum vulgare* (marjoram)
12. 1 *Lysimachia nummularia* 'Aurea'
13. 1 *Salvia officinalis* 'Tricolor' (variegate sage)
14. 1 *Tropaeolum majus* (nasturtium)
15. 1 *Chrysanthemum parthenium* (feverfew)
16. 1 *Allium schoenoprasum* (chives)

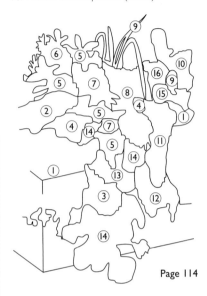

Page 114

Page 115 *Photographed early July*

CONTAINER
Type terracotta pot
Size height 15cm (6in), width 45cm (18in)

PLANTING
A permanent display of hardy perennial herbs.
Position sunny

Key to plants
1. 1 *Thymus pseudolanuginosus*
2. 1 *Thymus serpyllum* 'Pink Chintz'
3. 1 *Thymus serpyllum coccineus*
4. 1 *Thymus vulgaris* 'Silver Posie'
5. 1 *Thymus* x *citriodorus* 'Archer's Gold'

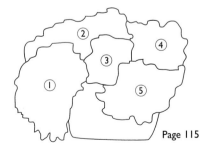

Page 115

Page 116 *Photographed late May*

CONTAINER
Type wire hanging basket
Size 35cm (14in)

PLANTING
Display of annual and biennial edible plants, raised under cover and planted out in spring.
Position sunny
Plants
3 tomato 'Tumbler'
7 *Petroselinum crispum* (parsley)

Page 117 *Photographed late May*

PLANTING
Annual fruiting plant raised under cover and planted out in the border in spring.
Position sunny
Plants 5 tomato 'Moneymaker'

CLASSIC FAVOURITES
Roses

Each type of rose differs substantially in the way it is pruned. Rambler roses are best pruned in late summer after flowering by cutting out the stems that have borne flowers, as near to the ground as possible. The new growth produced during the current year can then be tied into place. Climbers need to be trained to build up a permanent framework of main branches, and the lateral sideshoots only are pruned in late winter by cutting them back to within several buds of the main stem. Roses benefit from generous feeding. In spring top-dress with well-rotted manure or compost.

Page 118 *Photographed mid-June*

PLANTING
Mixed climbers growing permanently in a border. The clematis can be pruned in late winter at the same time as the rose.
Position sunny
Plants
Left 1 *Clematis* 'Perle d'Azur'
Right 1 *Rosa* 'Bantry Bay' climbing

Page 121 *Photographed late May*

CONTAINER
Type wire hanging basket
Size 30cm (12in)

PLANTING
Ground-cover roses growing in a hanging basket planted by Mattocks Roses. The plants can be kept in the same basket for several years by hard pruning in early spring and top-dressing with fresh compost and fertilizer (see page 140).
Position sunny
Plants 3 *Rosa* 'Suffolk'

Pages 122–3 *Photographed early July*

PLANTING

Rambler rose growing permanently in a border at David Austin Roses.
Position sunny
Plant 1 *Rosa* 'Paul's Himalayan Musk'

Page 123 *Photographed mid-June*

PLANTING

Weeping standard rambler roses and perennials shrubs planted in the border for permanent display.
Position sunny
Plants
Above 8 *Rosa* 'Sanders' White Rambler'
Below 30 *Lavandula angustifolia* 'Munstead'

Page 124 *Photographed mid-July*

PLANTING

Climbing rose growing in a border.
Position sunny
Plant 1 *Rosa* 'Chaplin's Pink Climber'

Page 125 above *Photographed mid-July*

PLANTING

Rambler rose growing in a border.
Position sunny
Plant 1 *Rosa* 'Félicité Perpétue'

Page 125 below *Photographed late June*

PLANTING

Climbing rose growing permanently in a border.
Position sunny
Plant 1 *Rosa* 'Blairii Number 2'

THE CHARM OF THE WILD
Wild flowers and natives

In containers and borders, wild flowers do best if they are given the same treatment as other garden plants. Wild flowers for containers should be planted in fresh potting compost as advised on page 139, and then fed, watered and deadheaded regularly, as for other seasonal plantings. They do benefit from occasional pinching-out of their shoot tips to encourage more bushy growth.

Page 126 *Photographed early August*

CONTAINER

Type terracotta wall pot
Size height 20cm (8in), width 30cm (12in)

PLANTING

A mixture of annuals and perennials for summer colour, created by Marney Hall of Countryside Wild Flowers. The trailing plants around the edge could remain in place when the annuals, poppies and pheasant's eye, are replaced in late summer.
Position sunny or part shade

Key to plants
1. 1 *Lotus corniculatus* (bird's-foot trefoil)
2. 1 *Adonis annua* (pheasant's eye)
3. 1 *Papaver rhoeas* (field poppy)
4. 1 *Centranthus ruber* (red valerian)
5. 1 *Viola tricolor* (wild pansy)
6. 1 *Lysimachia nummularia* (creeping Jenny)

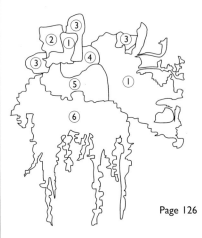

Page 126

Page 129 *Photographed early August*

CONTAINER

Type wire hanging basket
Size 35cm (14in)

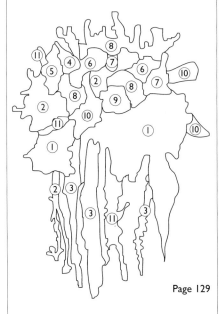

Page 129

PLANTING

A summer display of mixed perennials with annual pheasant's eye, created by Marney Hall. The trailing plants can remain in place all year.
Position sunny or part shade

Key to plants
1. 5 *Lysimachia nummularia* (creeping Jenny)
2. 1 *Lotus corniculatus* (bird's-foot trefoil)
3. 3 *Galium vernum* (lady's bedstraw)
4. 1 *Linaria vulgaris* (common toadflax)
5. 1 *Jasione montana* (sheep's-bit)
6. 1 *Adonis annua* (pheasant's eye)
7. 3 *Viola tricolor* (wild pansy)
8. 3 *Campanula rotundifolia* (harebell)
9. 3 *Fragaria vesca* (wild strawberry)
10. 1 *Geranium robertianum* (herb Robert)
11. 1 *Potentilla anserina* (silverweed)

Page 130 *Photographed early June*

PLANTING

Part of a rock garden with a hardy perennial evergreen cushion plant, also suitable for containers, raised beds and path or border edges.
Position sunny with well-drained soil
Plant 1 *Armeria maritima* (thrift, sea-pink)

Page 131 *Photographed mid-June*

PLANTING

This hardy perennial growing in a crevice of a dry-stone wall is also suitable for hanging baskets and other containers.
Position sunny or shade
Plant 1 *Cymbalaria muralis* (ivy-leaved toad flax)

Pages 132–3 *Photographed mid-May*

CONTAINER

Type an old bath
Size height 23cm (9 in), width 75cm (30in)

PLANTING

Herbaceous perennial easily grown from seed and ideal for crevice planting such as in dry-stone walls and cracks in paths. Once established it will self seed.
Position sunny or shade
Plants 5 *Corydalis lutea* (*Pseudofumaria lutea*) (yellow fumitory)

Page 134 *Photographed mid-March*

CONTAINER

Type terracotta wall pot
Size height 20cm (8in), width 23cm (9in)

PLANTING

A winter wall pot, planted with perennial evergreens by Marney Hall, to give interest from autumn to early spring. The wild pansy produces flowers sporadically even in winter, weather permitting.

Position sunny or partial shade
Plants
Above 3 *Viola tricolor* (wild pansy)
Below 1 *Thymus polytrichus* (*Thymus drucei*) (creeping thyme)

Pages 134–5 *Photographed mid-September*

PLANTING

Three pots planted by Marney Hall with herbaceous perennials for year-round effect. The pansies have been left to self-seed and colonize a corner of a gravel drive.
Position sunny or partial shade

CONTAINERS

Type 3 terracotta pots
Size height 23–38cm (9–15in), width 27–33cm (11–13in)

Key to plants
1. 5 *Viola tricolor* (wild pansy)
2. 1 *Fragaria vesca* (wild strawberry)
3. 3 *Lysimachia nummularia* (creeping Jenny)
4. 1 *Digitalis purpurea* (foxglove)

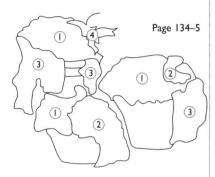

Page 134–5

Page 136 *Photographed early August*

GROUP PLANTING

A massed display of summer bedding plants in hanging baskets and pots, planted in spring and grown at the Woodman Inn, Durley, Hampshire, by landlord Tony Senger.
Position sunny

CONTAINER A

Type wooden half-barrel
Size height 38cm (15in), width 60cm (2ft)
Key to plants
1. 3 *Calceolaria integrifolia* 'Sunshine'
2. 3 *Argyranthemum* 'Royal Yellow'

CONTAINER B

Type individual plastic pots massed on the ground, some of which are sitting on others upturned
Size 10cm (4in)

Key to plants
3. 50 *Impatiens* 'Rose Star' and 'Super Elfin Swirl' plus 10 *Begonia* Non-stop Series

CONTAINER C

Type wooden half-barrel
Size height 38cm (15in), width 60cm (2ft)

Key to plants
4. 5 *Petunia* 'Express White' plus 7 *Pelargonium* zonal red and pink cvs.

CONTAINER D

Type window-box made from old scaffolding boards
Size length 1m (3ft 3in), width and height 20cm (8in)

Key to plants
5. 3 *Lobelia* 'Lilac Fountain'
6. 3 *Begonia* 'Non-stop Yellow'
7. 3 *Pelargonium* 'Rouletta'
8. 2 *Fuchsia* pink cv. trained as a bush
9. 3 *Begonia* 'Non-stop Pink'
10. 3 *Begonia* 'Non-stop Red'
11. 1 *Helichrysum petiolare* 'Roundabout'
12. 3 *Calceolaria integrifolia* 'Sunshine'
13. 3 *Impatiens* 'Accent Pink'

CONTAINER E

Type plastic pot
Size 18cm (7in)

Key to plant
14. 1 *Fuchsia* pale pink cv.

CONTAINER F

Type 2 wire hanging baskets
Size 40cm (16in)

Key to plants (baskets identical)
15. 3 *Pelargonium* 'Cherry Sundae'
16. 5 *Pelargonium* 'Tiberias'
17. 5 *Fuchsia* mixed trailing cvs.
18. 9 *Lobelia* Fountain Series

CONTAINER G

Type wire hanging basket
Size 40cm (16in)

Key to plants
19. 3 *Calceolaria integrifolia* 'Sunshine'
20. 3 *Pelargonium* 'Bruni'
21. 5 *Lobelia* Fountain Series
22. 3 *Fuchsia* mixed trailing cvs.
23. 5 *Pelargonium* 'Leucht Cascade'

Page 136

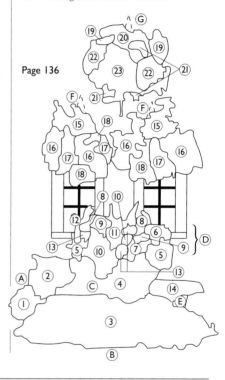

FURTHER READING

For gardening advice and ideas, I recommend:

Brown, L. *Vegetables for Small Gardens.* London: BBC Books, 1993.

Chatto, B. *The Green Tapestry.* London: Collins, 1989.

Hamilton, G. *The Ornamental Kitchen Garden.* London: BBC Books, 1991.

Hessayon, D. G. *The Bedding Plant Expert.* London: Expert Books, 1993. New York: Sterling Publishing Co, 1991.

Keeling, J. *The New Terracotta Gardener.* London: Headline, 1993. Vermont: Trafalgar Square Publishing, 1990.

Kingsbury, N. *The Wild Flower Garden.* London: Conran Octopus, 1994.

Llewelyn, R. *Elegance and Eccentricity.* London: Ward Lock, 1989.

McVicar, J. *Jekka's Complete Herb Book.* London: Kyle Cathie Ltd, 1994.

Taylor, J. *Creative Planting with Climbers.* London: Ward Lock, 1991. New York: Sterling Publishing Co, 1993.

Thomas, G. S. *Perennial Garden Plants or The Modern Floregium.* London: Dent, 3rd ed. 1990. Oregon: Timber Press, 1990.

The RHS Plant Finder
Ashbourne: Moorlands Publishing Co. Ltd.
Revised annually, this invaluable guide lists where you can buy over 60,000 plants.

In addition, the catalogues produced by specialist nurseries in particular often contain lots of information about plants and how to grow them. As well as the select List of Suppliers, look through the classified advertisements of gardening magazines, and in gardening show literature.

LIST OF SUPPLIERS

Great Britain

HANGING BASKETS

Erin Marketing Ltd
Knowsley Industrial Estate
Park North,
Kirksby, Liverpool L33 7SS
Tel 0151 549 2399
Fax 0151 548 3587

Gardman Ltd
Northgate, Pinchbeck
Spalding, Lincs PE11 3SQ
Tel 01775 766021
Fax 01775 710223

SWAGS

Westlanz Swags Ltd
Blaentir, Llangain
Carmarthen, Dyfed SA33 5AY
Tel/Fax 01267 241361

TERRACOTTA CONTAINERS

Shebbear Pottery
(Clive Bowen)
Shebbear, Devon EX21 5QZ
Tel 01409 281271

Whichford Pottery
Whichford, Shipston-on-Stour
Warwicks CV36 5PG
Tel 01608 684416
Fax 01608 684833

WICKER BASKETS

Adrian Charlton
1 Hall Cottage, Wood Lane
Burgh-next-Aylsham
Norfolk NR11 6TS
Tel 01263 734585

WATERING EQUIPMENT

Gardena UK Ltd
Dunhams Lane
Letchworth Garden City
Herts SG6 1BD
Tel 01462 686688
Fax 01462 686789

ORNAMENTAL WIRE CONTAINERS

James Gilbert & Son
129 The Vale, Acton
London W3 7RQ
Tel 0181 743 1566
Fax 0181 746 1393

Celestino Valenti,
Tuppence House
28 Watermoor Road
Cirencester, Glos GL7 1JW
Tel 01285 642583

WROUGHT-IRON JARDINIÈRES, HANGING BASKET STANDS, BASKETS, BRACKETS AND PLANTERS

Otter Wrought Iron Products
Unit 2, Clees Hall Workshops
Alphamstone, nr Bures
Suffolk CO8 5DZ
Tel 01787 228280
Fax 01787 228280
All designs are copyright

PLANTS

Bernwode Plants
The Thatched Cottage
Duck Lane, Ludgershall
Aylesbury, Bucks HP18 9NZ
Tel 01844 237415
Perennials, alpines and herbs

Brockings Exotics
Petherwin Gate
North Petherwin
Launceston
Cornwall PL15 8LW
Tel 01566 785533
Frost-tender perennials

Bressingham Gardens
Diss, Norfolk IP22 2AB
Tel 01379 687464
Fax 01379 688034
Perennials, ornamental grasses, alpines and climbers

Elm House Nursery
PO Box 25, Wisbech
Cambs PE13 2RR
Tel 01945 581511
Fax 01945 588235
Frost-tender perennials (young plants)

Fibrex Nurseries Ltd
Honeybourne Road, Pebworth
nr Stratford-on-Avon
Warwicks CV37 8XT
Tel 01789 720788
Ivies, ferns and pelargoniums

Heather and Brian Hiley
25 Little Woodcote Estate
Wallington, Surrey SM5 4AU
Tel 0181 647 9679
Frost-tender perennials
3 1st class stamps for a catalogue

P de Jager & Sons Ltd
Staplehurst Road
Marden, Kent TN12 9BP
Tel 01622 831235
Fax 01622 832416
Bulbs and tubers

Jekka's Herb Farm
Rose Cottage
Shellards Lane
Alveston, Bristol BS12 2SY
Tel/Fax 01454 418878
Herbs.
Large sae, 2 1st class stamps, for a catalogue

Mattocks Roses
The Rose Nursery
Nuneham Courtenay
Oxford OX44 9PY
Tel 01865 343265
Fax 01865 343267
Roses

Treasures of Tenbury Ltd
Burford, Tenbury Wells
Worcs WR15 8HQ
Tel 01584 810777
Fax 01584 810673
Clematis and other climbers

The Vernon Geranium Nursery
Cuddington Way, Cheam
Surrey SM2 7JB
Tel 0181 393 7616
Fax 0181 786 7437
Pelargoniums and fuchsias

United States

GENERAL

Smith & Hawken
25 Corte Madera
Mill Valley, CA 94941
Tel (415) 383 4050

Gardener's Eden
3250 Van Ness Avenue
San Francisco, CA 94109
Tel (415) 421 7900

HANGING BASKETS

OFE International Inc.
PO Box 161302
Miami, FL 33186
Tel (305) 253 7080

Plant Collectibles
103 Kenview Avenue
Buffalo, NY 14217
Tel (716) 875 1221

TERRACOTTA CONTAINERS

Hollyhock
214 North Larchmont Blvd
Los Angeles, CA 90004
Tel (213) 931 3400

Treillage
418 East 75th Street
New York, NY 10021
Tel (212) 535 2288

PLANTS

W Atlee Burpee Co.
300 Park Avenue
Warminster, PA 18974
Tel (215) 674 4900

DeGiorgi Seed Co.
6011 'N' Street
Omaha, NE 68117
Tel (402) 731 3901

Johnny's Selected Seeds
Foss Hill Road
Albion, ME 04910
Tel (207) 437 9294

J. W. Jung Seed Co.
335 S High Street
Randolph, WI 53957
Tel (414) 326 4100

Nicholas Garden Nursery Inc.
1190 N Pacific Highway
Albany, OR 97321
Tel (503) 928 9280

Park Seed Co.
Cokesbury Road
Greenwood, SC 29647
Tel (803) 223 7333

Shepherd's Garden Seeds
30 Irene Street
Torrington, CT 06790
Tel (800) 357 9092

Thompson & Morgan
PO Box 1308
Jackson, NJ 08527
Tel (800) 274 7333

Wayside Gardens
1 Garden Lane
Hodges, SC 29695
Tel (800) 845 1124

White Flower Farm
PO Box 50
Litchfield, CT 06759
Tel (203) 496 9600

INDEX

ACKNOWLEDGEMENTS

Many people were involved in the numerous stages of this book and together they contributed a great deal of time, enthusiasm, and hard work, whilst still retaining that essential attribute – a sense of humour. My thanks to them all: to Ian Jackson at Eddison Sadd for the original idea; to the growers and gardeners who allowed us to disrupt their days in order to take the photographs, and particularly to those people who put so much time, thought and expertise into creating displays especially for the book; to the suppliers who generously loaned their products; and to John Glover for his boundless flexibility and patience in taking all the wonderful photographs at so many different locations. For help and information researching the historical background for Part One, my thanks to David Blunden of James Gilbert & Sons and the staff at the Royal Horticultural Society's Lindley Library. At Eddison Sadd, I would like to thank Ian Jackson and Elaine Partington for steering me through the whole process of creating the book; to Pritty Ramjee for the design; and to Barbara Haynes for her sympathetic and knowledgeable editing.

Last but certainly not least, I would like to thank my husband Chris and my parents for their constant support and encouragement.

Picture Credits: Bridgeman Art Library 9; Mary Evans Picture Library 8; The Royal Horticultural Society, Lindley Library 11,12; David Blunden of Gilbert and Sons 13. All other photographs are by John Glover.

Editorial Director Ian Jackson
Editor Barbara Haynes
Proof Reader Tessa Monina
Indexer Dorothy Frame
Art Director Elaine Partington
Senior Designer Pritty Ramjee
Design Assistants Lynne Ross and Rachel Kirkland
Line-drawing Artist Anthony Duke
Production Hazel Kirkman and Charles James